Japanese Language Learning Guide for Travelers:

Easy way to learn Japanese for your Japan trip
* Plus 2 FREE gifts

Asuka Tsuchiya, Ph.D.

First Published 2015
Revised 2021

ISBN-13: 978-1512229134
ISBN-10: 151222913X

Cover illustration: 小咲さと Kosaki Sato
Proof-readers: Jacqui Mcginn, photorresrivero, speedy876

Bonus Audio producer: Hanae
Presenters: Kusa Chiaki, Kaza Midori, shun, Shige, Asuka

Welcome! Yōkoso! ようこそ

If you plan to go to Japan, or this is your first attempt at learning Japanese, or maybe you learned Japanese a long time ago and would like to refresh your Japanese, this book is for you.

Japanese Language Learning Guide for Travelers contains everything you need to effectively and efficiently communicate with local Japanese people during your trip to Japan.

Time is precious, especially if you are busy planning your trip, tackling lots of work before a holiday, and ensuring that everything is in place and will be okay while you are away. Even though you are interested in learning Japanese for your holiday, you may not have plenty of time for studying. You need an effective way to learn.

No worries. This book will help you.

This unique and easy-to-learn book **with 2 FREE gifts** focuses on the needs of travelers like you. With this book, you can learn practical Japanese quickly and easily, saving you time to prepare for your travel.

1st Secret of Success: Focusing on Practical Travel-Related Japanese

I think that we all have had some experience learning a foreign language in school or somewhere else.
How long did it take? One year? Two years? Or even a decade?
We all know it takes a long time to learn languages.

Then, how is it possible to learn Japanese quickly?

I would like to show you the 1st secret of success, **focusing on the outcome you want to achieve.**

As a tourist, your current goal is to communicate with local Japanese people **in Japanese** during your travel. What you need is travel-related Japanese, which actually works. You have no time to be distracted by school- or business-related Japanese, for example.

Japanese Language Learning Guide for Travelers covers 5 essential themes, getting to know each other, eating out, shopping, going out, and asking for help, which all travelers would be involved in from Day 1 of their trip. You will learn useful expressions and vocabulary which you can use every day during your stay in Japan. The easy-to-read grammar sections give you a good understanding of the Japanese language structure. You will also get practical and cultural information related to each theme.

After reading this book, you will be well informed of how to talk in Japanese.

2nd Secret of Success: Free gift #1 Audio Files

But you might wonder, "How can I talk? Listening and speaking are the most difficult part of language learning!"

Yes, you are right. Listening and speaking skills are challenging to attain, especially if you study Japanese by just READING a textbook. You definitely need to LISTEN.

Here comes the 2nd secret of success. **The special FREE gift #1, Full Audio Files**, recorded by **100% genuine Japanese native speakers.**

The Audio Files cover ALL the main dialogues, ALL key sentences, ALL speaking practices, ALL listening practices, and more! You can listen to an enormous amount of good quality spoken Japanese. You can practice plenty of listening and speaking exercises, which will help you gain good listening and speaking skills. As we all know, these skills are vital for communication.

The files are in mp3 format, so you can download them in your favorite mp3 player and listen to them anytime and anywhere you like.

Using this free gift, you can speak in Japanese with confidence.

3rd Secret of Success: Free Gift #2 Ready-Made Anki e-Flash Cards with Audio

"But," you might still think, "How about vocabulary? I have struggled to memorize words when I learn a new language. My memory is rubbish."

A vast vocabulary is also a vital element of good communication. However, all of us know it is a tough job to memorize new words.

Here is the 3rd secret of success: **the exceptional FREE gift #2, Ready-Made Anki e-Flash Cards with Audio.**

These e-flash cards cover ALL words and ALL key sentences in this book. You do not need to create flash cards from scratch. Everything is ready for you. You can start immediately.

These cards also contain audio. You can listen to the proper pronunciation and repeat it aloud each time you use the cards. It will assist you in remembering how to pronounce the words and the key sentences so that you can use them confidently.

All you have to do is download the Anki app on your laptop, tablet, or smartphone and use these e-flash cards every day for just 3 minutes or less. Anki enables you to learn new words by spaced repetition, which is the most effective method to memorize words and retain them for a long time. If you have not remembered a particular word sufficiently, Anki will show it to you again within a few minutes. If you have already memorized it, this app will make it come up again a few days later. So there is no way that the words and the phrases should escape memory. I will explain how to use the Anki app later in this book.

With these e-flash cards, your brain absorbs all the words and the key sentences. You can memorize them and recall them quickly.

A bit of Adventure: Reading Hiragana and Katakana

If you would like to explore the Japanese language world more, I will give you a bit of adventure, **Reading Hiragana and Katakana**.

I have been aware that many tourists are fascinated by these strange-looking Japanese Letters. It might be fun if you spot them during your trip, so I will show you how to read them. Give it a try!

Success is almost within Your Grasp: Let's Learn Together to Make Your Journey Special!

Japanese Language Learning Guide for Travelers and with **2 Free special gifts**, you can learn Japanese, listen to Japanese, speak Japanese, practice Japanese and memorize Japanese quickly and easily.

Learning a new language and communicating with local people would be a life-changing experience. Following this book, audio files, and e-flash cards, you will be well prepared. You will avoid any regret like "I should have learned more before I came to Japan!" You can chat with people and explore Japan full of confidence. After the great adventure, you will get tons of unforgettable memories (and countless pictures, perhaps). It's wonderful, isn't it?

Are you ready to learn? If your answer is "Yes," let's go together!

Dr. Asuka Tsuchiya

Southampton, UK 2015

FREE Gifts for YOU!

As I mentioned above, I would like to offer you special free gifts exclusive to the readers.

The complete Audio Files and the Ready-Made Anki e-Flash Cards will help you learn Japanese effectively. To get the maximum effect from this book, I recommend getting these gifts from the link below:

http://www.funjapaneselearning.com/travelersfreegifts

How to use this book

Are you excited? Great! Now, please let me show you how this book works.

This book contains these sections:

Dialogues: The main story of this book is Ms. Smith's trip to Japan. She experiences 5 essential themes which most tourists get involved in – getting to know each other, eating out, shopping, going out, and asking for help. Following her story, you can virtually experience each situation and learn practical and valuable expressions which work wonderfully. Listen to the **Audio Files** and find out what is happening. You will learn key sentences and new words in a context. You will get good examples of how to communicate with people.

Grammar and Expressions: You can learn Japanese grammar and expressions in a friendly, approachable way as if your personal teacher is sitting next to you. Read through this section to grasp the Japanese language structure. Using the **Audio files**, you can listen to the sample Japanese sentences. This basic grammar will give you a solid foundation of basic Japanese. You can make an excellent start to Japanese learning, making it easier to go forward to learn advanced Japanese in the future if you would like to continue.

Practice Dialogues: In this speaking practice, you will take one of the character's roles. Using the **Audio Files**, you can speak the character's lines and virtually "chat" with other characters. Through this exercise, you will quickly learn each sentence by heart. It will improve your speaking ability and boost your confidence.

Related Vocabulary: Vocabulary is essential for communication. You can express yourself and be understood if you know the words, even though the sentence you compose is not so perfect. In this book, you will learn lots of related words. Please remember that you can memorize all of them without any hassle. Download free gift, **Anki e-Flash Cards with Audio,** and use them regularly!

Speaking Practice: This section provides you with the opportunity to speak by yourself, using your own knowledge; it will improve your speaking skill dramatically. Speak aloud. Expand key phrases. You will find you can say what you want to say. Through this exercise, you can communicate smoothly. **Audio files** provide you the spoken answers so you can listen to them and repeat them aloud. It will help you speak like native Japanese.

Listening Practice: In this section, you use **Audio Files** and listen to the audio recordings **spoken by 100% genuine native Japanese presenters**. Listen to the audio carefully and write down your answer. These audio exercises will improve your listening skill dramatically. When you are in Japan, you will find you can understand what people say.

Further practice: This section contains a variety of exercises. It helps you put all the information you have learned together. You can "digest" your knowledge and use it well. You can listen to the spoken answers by the **Audio Files,** so you also practice listening and speaking. Your learning curve will go up steeply!

Hiragana and Katakana Reading Quiz (optional): Although you don't have to read Japanese letters during your trip, I suppose you might be interested in a bit of adventure, so that I will provide you the optional reading exercises. If you would like to do so, Please go this way. Firstly, read Chapter 0, which gives you a good overview of the Japanese writing system. Secondly, do Hiragana and Katakana Reading Quiz in each chapter. Third, listen to the answers by **Audio Files**. I hope you enjoy it.

Key sentences: In this section, you will revise practical sentences in each chapter. Your **Anki e-Flash Cards with Audio** include ALL key sentences. Using these e-Flash Cards, you can use essential key sentences correctly and confidently.

Cultural Information: As you are going to Japan, you would be interested in Japanese culture. This section shows you practical tips on Japanese culture and customs, which are helpful for tourists like you. Reading through this section, you will be informed how to behave appropriately, which shows your understanding and respect for Japanese culture. You will be appreciated by local Japanese people.

Answers: All the answers are provided at the end of the book. You can listen to ALL the answers by **Audio Files**. English translations are also provided if required. You can self-study confidently.

Japanese-English, English-Japanese Glossaries: At the end of the book, there are Japanese-English, English-Japanese glossaries, which show all the words in this book. If you would like to check a particular word, you can easily find it.

Free Gifts:

This is the Audio Icon. It indicates which file you should listen to. Open your **Audio Files** with your favorite mp3 player and listen to them.

This is the Deck Icon. It indicates which deck (set of flash cards) you should work with. Open your **e-Flash Cards** with the **Anki** app and use them regularly.

With the *Japanese Language Learning Guide for Travelers*, **Audio Files,** and **e-Flash Cards**, you have already been well equipped and ready to learn Japanese.

Let's start learning Japanese!

Table of contents

Chapter 0. Writing and Pronunciation

Before we go, let's have a quick look at Japanese writing systems.

Japanese Writing Systems

The Japanese language has three writing systems.

- Kanji: Chinese characters which came from China and developed in Japan. Kanji conveys meanings.
- Hiragana: Phonetic letters
- Katakana: Phonetic letters which are used to write foreign origin words.

Japanese is usually written in these three writing systems together. Here is an example:

スミスさんはイギリス人ですか。
Sumisu san wa igirisu jin desu ka.

Are you British, Ms. Smith?

人 is Kanji. さん, は, です and か are Hiragana. スミス and イギリス are Katakana.

"Sumisu san wa igirisu jin desu ka." is Rōmaji, the letters of the Roman alphabet. Rōmaji is not used in standard Japanese scripts but useful for learners because it is easy to pronounce.

In this book, Rōmaji is mainly used since it is convenient to read. However, I also show you Kanji, Hiragana, and Katakana.

Hiragana and Katakana are relatively easy to learn. They are phonetic, so once you get to know them, you can read! Each of them consists of basic 46 letters plus some extra. Later in this chapter, you can find Hiragana and Katakana letter tables. I also offer you some Hiragana and Katakana reading exercises. These are totally optional, so please don't worry. But if you get to be familiar with them, it would be nice.

If you want to learn Hiragana and Katakana more, please check my book:
Complete Japanese Hiragana: ISBN 978-1-914249-00-6
Complete Japanese Katakana: ISBN 978-1-914249-09-9

Learning Kanji is a huge task. There are about 2,000 characters for everyday use. It is far beyond what this little book can deal with, so I won't give you Kanji exercises but show you Kanji in the dialogue to immerse you in the Japanese text. You can get used to Kanji.

Here is how Japanese is written in this book. I show you the Rōmaji script and Japanese script, Kanji, Hiragana, and Katakana, in the dialogue section. I put Hiragana on top of each Kanji to show how to read, so you do not need to be scared! In other sections, I use Hiragana and Katakana to make the Japanese script easy to read and give you plenty of opportunities to practice.

Font

In this book, "**Kyōkasho tai** きょうかしょたい" font is used. "Kyōkasho tai," literary means "textbook font," is based on traditional Japanese handwriting. This font helps learners to understand how to write Japanese letters and characters accurately.

In Japan, the "Kyōkasho tai" font is used to teach the Japanese language to Japanese children in all elementary schools. Japanese Language Proficiency Test (JLPT), the most established Japanese language test, uses this font for beginners' level because it is vital for beginners to learn the exact shape of Japanese letters and characters. Unfortunately, this font is not commonly used in digital devices, so most non-Japanese teachers and publishers don't use it.

When you type Japanese words on digital devices, fonts called Mincho and Gothic usually appear. Even though these fonts are designed nicely, the shapes are inappropriate to copy when you learn how to write.

Here is an example, Hiragana " り **ri**" written in three different fonts.

Mincho	Gothic	Kyōkasho tai
り	り	り

By Mincho font, the letter "ri" looks as if one long zigzag line. By Gothic font, you can see two lines, but they look too straight and rigid. "Kyōkasho tai" shows you the required curves of this letter perfectly and beautifully.

In this book, only "Kyōkasho tai" is used so you can attain better handwriting!

Hiragana and Katakana

Here are the Japanese letter tables. Each cell represents one sound and 3 different ways of writing, Rōmaji, Hiragana, and Katakana. Please listen to the mp3 files to learn proper pronunciation.

🎧 Track0-1

	a あア	i いイ	u うウ	e えエ	o おオ
k	ka かカ	ki きキ	ku くク	ke けケ	ko こコ
s	sa さサ	shi しシ	su すス	se せセ	so そソ
t	ta たタ	chi ちチ	tsu つツ	te てテ	to とト
n	na なナ	ni にニ	nu ぬヌ	ne ねネ	no のノ
h	ha はハ	hi ひヒ	fu ふフ	he へヘ	ho ほホ
m	ma まマ	mi みミ	mu むム	me めメ	mo もモ
y	ya やヤ		yu ゆユ		yo よヨ
r	ra らラ	ri りリ	ru るル	re れレ	ro ろロ
w	wa わワ				wo をヲ
n	n んン				

🎧 Track0-2

g	ga がガ	gi ぎギ	gu ぐグ	ge げゲ	go ごゴ
z	za ざザ	ji じジ	zu ずズ	ze ぜゼ	zo ぞゾ
d	da だダ	ji ぢヂ	zu づヅ	de でデ	do どド
b	ba ばバ	bi びビ	bu ぶブ	be べベ	bo ぼボ
p	pa ぱパ	pi ぴピ	pu ぷプ	pe ぺペ	po ぽポ

🎧 Track0-3

ky	kya きゃ キャ	kyu きゅ キュ	kyo きょ キョ
sh	sha しゃ シャ	shu しゅ シュ	sho しょ ショ
ch	cha ちゃ チャ	chu ちゅ チュ	cho ちょ チョ
ny	nya にゃ ニャ	nyu にゅ ニュ	nyo にょ ニョ
hy	hya ひゃ ヒャ	hyu ひゅ ヒュ	hyo ひょ ヒョ
my	mya みゃ ミャ	my みゅ ミュ	myo みょ ミョ
ry	rya りゃ リャ	ryu りゅ リュ	ryo りょ リョ

🎧 Track0-4

gy	gya ぎゃ ギャ	gyu ぎゅ ギュ	gyo ぎょ ギョ
j	ja じゃ ジャ	ju じゅ ジュ	jo じょ ジョ
by	bya びゃ ビャ	byu びゅ ビュ	byo びょ ビョ
py	pya ぴゃ ピャ	pyu ぴゅ ピュ	pyo ぴょ ピョ

Long vowel

Long vowels mean the vowels are doubled in length.

In Rōmaji, long vowels of **a**, **u**, **e** and **o** are shown as adding a bar (–) on top of the letter, like **ā**, **ū**, **ē** and **ō**. For **i** sound, simply one more **i** letter is added, like **ii**.

In Hiragana, usually, the vowel of the first letter is added. For example, the vowel of "ka か" is "a あ," so "kā" is written as "かあ." However, "ō" is a bit tricky. "Ō" is generally written as the letter "**u** う" added. For example, "**otōsan** (father)" is written as "おとうさん" But there are several exceptions which are written as "o お" added. For example, "**ōkii** (big)" is "おおきい."

In Katakana, a bar (-) is added between letters. For example, "**pūru** (pool)" is "プール."

Small "tsu つ"

Small "**tsu** つ" means you should hold your breath and be silent as long as one syllable length.

In Rōmaji, a consonant after silence is written twice, like "**kitte** (stamp)."

In Hiragana or Katakana, small "**tsu** つ" is used, like "きって"

Comma and Period

In the Rōmaji script, the comma and period are written the same as in English.

In Japanese script, the comma is written as "、" and the period as "。".

Extra sounds only for Katakana

Since Katakana represents the sounds of foreign words, there are several extra sounds only for Katakana. For example, "party" is written as "**pātii** パーティー," "fork" is "**fōku** フォーク" and "chess" is "**chesu** チェス." Here is the table.

 Track0-5

	a	i	u	e	o
y				ye イェ	
w		wi ウィ		we ウェ	wo ウォ
kw	kwa クァ	kwi クィ		kwe クェ	kwo クォ
gw	gwa グァ	gwi グィ		gwe グェ	gwo グォ
ky				kye キェ	
sh				she シェ	
j				je ジェ	
s		si スィ			
z		zi ズィ			
ch				che チェ	
ts	tsa ツァ	tsi ツィ		tse ツェ	tso ツォ
t		ti ティ	tu トゥ		
d		di ディ	du ドゥ		
ty			tyu テュ		
dy			dyu デュ		
ny				nye ニェ	
hy				hye ヒェ	
f	fa ファ	fi フィ		fe フェ	fo フォ

v	va ヴァ	vi ヴィ	vu ヴ	ve ヴェ	vo ヴォ
fy			fyu フュ		fyo フョ
vy			vyu ヴュ		vyo ヴョ

At the end of each chapter, I will give you some optional reading quizzes. If you would like to give it a try, please enjoy it!

Chapter 1. Getting to know each other

When you arrive in Japan, you may find someone who welcomes you. It might be your new colleagues or your Japanese friends. In any case, wouldn't it be great to greet them in Japanese and introduce yourself?

In this chapter, you will learn how to

- Introduce yourself
- Introduce your friend to a Japanese person
- Start a conversation and get to know each other!

The main character in the dialogues in this book is Ms. Smith, or "Sumisu san (スミスさん)" in Japanese. We'll explore Japan with her.

Narita Airport

Dialogue 1: Are you Ms. Cole? Kōru san desu ka.

🎧 Track1-1

Ms. Smith is waiting for her new Japanese colleague at the airport. A woman mistakes her for someone else. She seems to look for the other person. How do you answer "yes" or "no" in Japanese? Let's find out.

Kūkō de

Onna no hito	Ano, sumimasen.
Sumisu	Hai.
Onna no hito	Kōru san desu ka.
Sumisu	Iie, chigaimasu.
Onna no hito	A, sumimasen.

くうこう
空港 で

おんな 女 のひと	あの、すみません。
スミス	はい。
おんな 女 のひと	コールさんですか。
スミス	いいえ、ちがいます。
おんな 女 のひと	あ、すみません。

At the airport

Woman	Excuse me.
Smith	Yes.
Woman	Are you Ms Cole?
Smith	No, I'm not.
Woman	Oh, sorry.

Vocabulary ☐Deck1

kūkō airport **ano** ah   **sumimasen** excuse me   **hai** yes
san   Mr, Mrs, Ms, Miss (add after a person's name)   **ka**
(question marker)   **iie** no   **chigaimasu** that's wrong

Grammar and Expressions
🎧 Track1-2

1. Are you...?   *Yes/No*

In this dialogue, a woman asks Ms. Smith:

Kōru san desu ka. コールさんですか。

Are you Ms. Cole?

"**San** さん" is similar to Mr. Ms. Miss, etc. in English, but
added after the name of the person, like "**Kōru san** コールさ
ん." It shows your respect for other people. That is why you
cannot put "**san** さん" next to your own name.

"**Ka** か" is a word that forms a question. We call these kinds of
small words "particles."

Particles cannot work independently but work as attached
after words. Some particles show how the previous part links
to the other parts of a sentence. Others add some meanings
or emotions. We will learn some fundamental particles in this
book.

"**Ka** か" is added to the end of a sentence and indicates a
question.

The basic answer is like this:
Hai. はい。   Yes. / **Iie.** いいえ。   No.

If you would like to add a bit and could more sophisticated, you can say:

Hai, sō desu.   はい、そうです。   Yes, that's right.

Iie, chigaimasu.   いいえ、ちがいます。   No, that's not right.

Practice Dialogue 1

 Track1-3

Now, let's practice this dialogue. At first, you will be Onna no hito.

Kūkō de

Onna no hito	(Say "excuse me")
Sumisu	Hai.
Onna no hito	(Ask "Are you Ms Cole?")
Sumisu	Iie, chigaimasu.
Onna no hito	(Say "sorry")

Did you manage it? Well Done!
Now you will be Sumisu san.

Kūkō de

Onna no hito	Ano, sumimasen.
Sumisu	(Say "yes")
Onna no hito	Kōru san desu ka.
Sumisu	(Say "No, I'm not")
Onna no hito	A, sumimasen.

How did you feel? Now you can ask a person's name and answer "yes." Great progress!

Dialogue 2: How do you do?　Hajimemashite.

🎧 Track1-4

Ms. Smith is still waiting for her new colleague when a gentleman speaks to her.

Yamada	Ano, Sumisu san desu ka.
Sumisu	Hai, Sumisu desu.
Yamada	Hajimemashite. Yamada desu.
Sumisu	Hajimemashite. Sumisu desu. Dōzo yoroshiku onegaishimasu.

山田 （やまだ）	あの、スミスさんですか。
スミス	はい、スミスです。
山田 （やまだ）	はじめまして。山田です。
スミス	はじめまして。スミスです。どうぞよろしくお願いします。

Yamada	Excuse me, are you Ms Smith?
Smith	Yes, I'm Smith.
Yamada	How do you do. I'm Yamada.
Smith	How do you do. I'm Smith. Nice to meet you.

Vocabulary 🗂 Deck1

hajimemashite　how do you do

dōzo yoroshiku onegaishimasu　nice to meet you　(You can leave out "dōzo")

Grammar and Expressions

🎧 Track1-5

1. I am ...

In this dialogue, Ms. Smith said: "**Sumisu desu.**スミスです。" which means "I am Smith."

Sumisu desu. スミスです。   I am Smith.

Yamada desu. やまだです。   I am Yamada.

As you can see, there is no "I" in these Japanese sentences. "I" or "You" is not usually mentioned if it is obvious from the context.

2. How to ask questions

Now, compare the sentences below.

Sumisu desu. スミスです。   I am Smith.

Sumisu san desu ka.　スミスさんですか。

Are you Ms/Mr/Miss Smith?

To ask questions in Japanese is very easy. You do not need to change the word order or put other words like "do" or "did" in English. As we learned, "**ka** か" indicates a question. So you just put "**ka** か" at the end of the sentence and, voila! You've managed to compose a question! Good news, isn't it?

Practice Dialogue 2

 Track1-6

It is the time to practice. First, you will be Sumisu san.

Yamada	Ano, Sumisu san desu ka.
Sumisu	(Say "yes, I am Smith.")
Yamada	Hajimemashite. Yamada desu.
Sumisu	(Say "how do you do. I am Smith. Nice to meet you.")

All right? Then let's try to be Yamada san.

Yamada	(Ask "Are you Ms Smith?")
Sumisu	Hai, Sumisu desu.
Yamada	(Say "How do you do. I am Yamada.")
Sumisu	Hajimemashite. Sumisu desu. Dōzo yoroshiku onegaishimasu.

Well done!

Dialogue 3: Are you American? Amerika jin desu ka.

🎧 Track1-7

Yamada san introduces his friend to Sumisu san, and Sumisu san start chatting with her.

Yamada	Sumisu san, kochira wa Kobayashi san desu. Watashi no tomodachi desu.
Kobayashi	Hajimemashite. Kobayashi desu. Sakura daigaku no gakusei desu. Yoroshiku onegaishimasu.
Sumisu	Hajimemashite. Sumisu desu. Gōrudo ginkō de hataraite imasu. Yoroshiku onegaishimasu.
Kobayashi	Sumisu san wa Amerika jin desu ka.
Sumisu	Iie, Igirisu jin desu.
Kobayashi	Sō desu ka. Rondon kara kimashita ka.
Sumisu	Iie, Sausanputon kara kimashita.
Kobayashi	Sō desu ka.

山田	スミスさん、こちらは 小林 さんです。私 のともだちです。
小林	はじめまして。小林 です。さくら大学の 学生です。よろしくお 願いします。
スミス	はじめまして。スミスです。ゴールド銀行で 働 いています。よろしくお 願いします。
小林	スミスさんはアメリカ 人ですか。
スミス	いいえ、イギリス 人です。

こばやし 小林	そうですか。ロンドンから来ました か。
スミス	いいえ、サウサンプトンから来まし た。
こばやし 小林	そうですか。

Yamada	Ms. Smith, this is Ms. Kobayashi. She is my friend.
Kobayashi	How do you do? I am Kobayashi. I am a student at Sakura University. Nice to meet you.
Smith	How do you do? I am Smith. I work for Gold Bank. Nice to meet you.
Kobayashi	Are you American, Ms. Smith?
Smith	No, I am British.
Kobayashi	I see. Are you from London?
Smith	No. I'm from Southampton.
Kobayashi	I see.

Vocabulary ☐ Deck1

kochira this (polite)　**wa** (particle that denotes the topic of a sentence)　**watashi** I　**no** of (particle indicating possession)　**tomodachi** friend　**daigaku** university　**gakusei** student **ginkō** bank　**de** (particle indicating the location where an action takes place)　**hataraite imasu** be working　**Amerika** America　**jin** (person from)　**Igirisu** the U.K.　**sō desu ka** I see　**kara** from (particle indicating origin or point of departure)　**kimashita** came　**kimasu** come

Grammar and Expressions

🎧 Track1-8

1. The particle "wa は"

In this dialogue, Yamada san says,

Kochira wa Kobayashi san desu.

こちらはこばやしさんです。

This is Ms. Kobayashi.

In this sentence, a particle "**wa** は" is attached to "**kochira** こちら (this)." The particle "**wa** は" indicates the topic of the sentence.

Usually, "**wa**" is written as "わ" in Hiragana, but this "**wa**" particle is written as "は."

Yamada san shows Ms. Smith a new topic, the other person, whose name is Kobayashi san.

When you introduce your friend, use this key sentence.

Kochira wa A san desu. こちらは A さんです。

This is Mr/Ms/Miss A.

2. The particle "no の"

Yamada san said, "**Watashi no tomodachi** わたしのともだち," which means "a friend **of** mine." Kobayashi san said, "**Sakura daigaku no gakusei desu.** さくらだいがくのがくせいです。". It means "I am a student **of** Sakura University."

The particle "**no** の" is used like "of" in English. Please be aware of the word order!

watashi (A) <u>**no**</u> **tomodachi** (B) = a friend (B) **of** mine (A)
daigaku (A) <u>**no**</u> **gakusei** (B) = a student (B) **of** a university (A)
A no (の) B = B of A

3. Occupation

When you meet someone for the first time, to mention your occupation may be a good place to start the conversation. If you would like to say, "I am a teacher," "I am a lawyer," or "I am a singer," you use the same sentence structure you used to give your name.

Enjinia desu.　エンジニアです。　I am an engineer.

*enjinia, engineer

(Occupation) desu.　(Occupation)です。I am (occupation).

It's simple, isn't it? I will give you a list of job titles shortly. Hopefully, you can find yours in it.

There is another expression to describe your job. Smith san said:

Gōrudo ginkō de hataraite imasu.
ゴールドぎんこうではたらいています。

I work for Gold Bank.

"**De** で" is a particle which indicates the location of an action. It is similar to English "in" or "at."

(Job place/ company name) de hataraite imasu.
(Job place/ company name)ではたらいています。
I work for (job place/ company name)

4. I'm from...

The next most common topic is your nationality or the place you came from. In the dialogue, Kobayashi san asked Ms. Smith about her nationality.

Sumisu san wa Amerika jin desu ka.

スミスさんはアメリカじんですか。

Are you American, Ms. Smith?

Bear in mind that Kobayashi san used Ms. Smith's name, not "you." We have the word which means "You," of course ("**anata** あなた"), but we don't use it so often. Usually, the listener's name is used.

Ms. Smith says,

Igirisu jin desu. イギリスじんです。 I am British.

(Country name) jin desu.   (Country name)じんです。

I'm (nationality).

If you would like to say your country or your hometown rather than your nationality, the expression "**kara kimashita** からきました"is for you. "**Kara** から" is also a particle that means "from." "**Kimashita** きました" means "came." So "**kara kimashita** からきました" literally means "I came from" in Japanese.

Rondon kara kimashita. ロンドンからきました。

I'm from London.

(Country or hometown) kara kimashita.

(Country or hometown)からきました。

I'm from (country or hometown).

Practice Dialogue 3

 Track1-9

We have learned a lot in this dialogue. To make sure you can use your new knowledge, let's practice now. You will take Yamada san and Sumisu san's part.

Yamada	(Call Ms. Smith and say, "this is Miss Kobayashi. She is a friend of mine.")
Kobayashi	Hajimemashite. Kobayashi desu. Sakura daigaku no gakusei desu. Yoroshiku onegaishimasu.
Sumisu	(Greet her and tell her your name. Say "I work for Gold Bank. Nice to meet you.")
Kobayashi	Sumisu san wa Amerika jin desu ka.
Sumisu	(Say no and tell her "I am British.")
Kobayashi	Sō desu ka. Rondon kara kimashita ka.
Sumisu	(Say no and tell her "I came from Southampton.")
Kobayashi	Sō desu ka.

Please take Kobayashi san's part.

Yamada	Sumisu san, kochira wa Kobayashi san desu. Watashi no tomodachi desu.
Kobayashi	(Greet her and tell her your name. Say "I am a student of Sakura University. Nice to meet you.")
Sumisu	Hajimemashite. Sumisu desu. Gōrudo ginkō de hataraite imasu. Yoroshiku onegaishimasu.
Kobayashi	(Ask Ms. Smith whether she is American or not.)
Sumisu	Iie, Igirisu jin desu.
Kobayashi	(Say "I see" and ask her whether she came from London.)
Sumisu	Iie, Sausanputon kara kimashita.
Kobayashi	(Say, "I see.")

Related Vocabulary 🖳 Deck1

Basic Greetings

🎧 Track1-10

During your stay in Japan, you will have plenty of opportunities to greet Japanese persons. Have you already listened to some of them?

Good morning	**Ohayō gozaimasu** おはようございます
Hello	**Konnichiwa** こんにちは
Good evening	**Konbanwa** こんばんは
Good night	**Oyasumi nasai** おやすみなさい
Good bye	**Sayōnara** さようなら
Excuse me	**Sumimasen** すみません
Thank you	**Arigatō gozaimasu** ありがとうございます
You're welcome	**Dō itashimashite** どういたしまして

Job titles

🎧 Track1-11

Here is the list of job titles.

teacher	**sensei** せんせい 先生
student	**gakusei** がくせい 学生
company employee	**kaishain** かいしゃいん 会社員
bank clerk	**ginkōin** ぎんこういん 銀行員
medical doctor	**isha** いしゃ 医者
engineer	**enjinia** エンジニア

researcher	**kenkyūsha** けんきゅうしゃ 研究者
secretary	**hisho** ひしょ　秘書
lawyer	**bengoshi** べんごし　弁護士
hairdresser	**biyōshi** びようし　美容師
police officer	**keisatsukan** けいさつかん 警察官
driver	**untenshu** うんてんしゅ 運転手
politician	**seijika** せいじか　政治家
painter	**gaka** がか　画家
musician	**ongakuka** おんがくか 音楽家
author	**sakka** さっか　作家
singer	**kashu** かしゅ　歌手
architect	**kenchikuka** けんちくか 建築家
shop clerk	**tenin** てんいん　店員
housewife	**shufu** しゅふ　主婦

If you would like to add more information, use "**no** の."

Student of Asama University
Asama daigaku no gakusei
あさまだいがくのがくせい　あさま大学の学生

Nurse of Machida hospital　**Machida byōin no kangoshi**
まちだびょういんのかんごし　町田病院の看護師

An employee of Toyosan **Toyosan no shain** トヨサンのしゃいん　トヨサンの社員 *When you say "employee of (company name)," not "**kaishain**" but "**shain**" is used.

Country and Nationality

🎧 Track1-12

Here is the word list for the name of the country and nationality. As you can see, nationality is country name plus "**jin** じん."

Australia	Ōsutoraria オーストラリア	Ōsutoraria jin オーストラリアじん
Austria	Ōsutoria オーストリア	Ōsutoria jin オーストリアじん
Brazil	Burajiru ブラジル	Burajiru jin ブラジルじん
Canada	Kanada カナダ	Kanada jin カナダじん
China	Chūgoku 中国　ちゅうごく	Chūgoku jin 中国人　ちゅうごくじん
The Czech Republic	Cheko チェコ	Cheko jin チェコじん
Egypt	Ejiputo エジプト	Ejiputo jin エジプトじん
France	Furansu フランス	Furansu jin フランスじん
Germany	Doitsu ドイツ	Doitsu jin ドイツじん
Hong Kong	Honkon 香港　ほんこん	Honkon jin 香港人　ほんこんじん
India	Indo インド	Indo jin インドじん
Indonesia	Indoneshia インドネシア	Indoneshia jin インドネシアじん
Ireland	Airurando アイルランド	Airurando jin アイルランドじん
Italy	Itaria イタリア	Itaria jin イタリアじん
Japan	Nihon 日本　にほん	Nihon jin 日本人　にほんじん

Mexico	**Mekishiko** メキシコ	**Mekishiko jin** メキシコじん
The Netherlands	**Oranda** オランダ	**Oranda jin** オランダじん
New Zealand	**Nyūjiirando** ニュージーランド	**Nyūjiirando jin** ニュージーランドじん
Russia	**Roshia** ロシア	**Roshia jin** ロシアじん
Singapore	**Shingapōru** シンガポール	**Shingapōru jin** シンガポールじん
South Korea	**Kankoku** 韓国　かんこく	**Kankoku jin** 韓国人　かんこくじん
Spain	**Supein** スペイン	**Supein jin** スペインじん
Sweden	**Suwēden** スウェーデン	**Suwēden jin** スウェーデンじん
Switzerland	**Suisu** スイス	**Suisu jin** スイスじん
Thailand	**Tai** タイ	**Tai jin** タイじん
United Kingdom	**Igirisu** イギリス	**Igirisu jin** イギリスじん
United States	**Amerika** アメリカ	**Amerika jin** アメリカじん

You might be realized that we try to mimic the sound of the country name in the native language. For example, Germany is "Deutschland" in German, so we call it "**Doitsu.**" Well, it isn't so bad, is it?

If you would like to mention your hometown in Japanese, the same rule is applied. Say the name of the place in the local language VERY SLOWLY. It usually works!

Speaking practice

 Track1-13

1. Introduce yourself

Now you can introduce yourself using these sentences.

How do you do?	**Hajimemashite.** はじめまして。
I am (your name).	**(your name) desu.**
	(your name) です。
I am (your nationality).	**(your nationality) desu.**
	(your nationality) です。
I came from (place).	**(place) kara kimashita.**
	(place) からきました。
I am (your job title).	**(your job title) desu.**
	(your job title) です。
I work for (company's name)	
	(company's name) de hataraite imasu.
	(company's name) ではたらいています。
Nice to meet you.	**Yoroshiku onegaishimasu.**
	よろしくおねがいします。

Miss Kinoshita will introduce herself to you.

Hajimemashite. Kinoshita desu. Nihon jin desu. Nagoya kara kimashita. Isha desu. Yoroshiku onegaishimasu.

はじめまして。きのしたです。にほんじんです。なごやか らきました。いしゃです。よろしくおねがいします。

Did you understand? Yes, Kinoshita san is Japanese and came from Nagoya. She is a medical doctor. Well done!

Next, it's your turn to introduce yourself! Please say aloud. You can write down your answer if you would like.

2. Introduce your friend to the other person

Imagine you would like to introduce your friend to the other person. You will use these sentences.

This is Mr/Ms/MissA.	**Kochira wa A san desu.**
	こちらは A さんです。
He/She is (nationality).	**A san wa (nationality) desu.**
	A さんは (nationality) です。
He/She came from (place).	**(place) kara kimashita.**
	(place) からきました。
He/She is (occupation).	**(occupation) desu.**
	(occupation) です。
He/She works for (company name).	
	(company name) de hataraite imasu.
	(company name) ではたらいています。

Could you introduce these people in the table below? I show you the non-Japanese name in Rōmaji in parentheses.

	name	nationality	hometown	occupation
ex)	Matsuda	Japanese	Chiba	company employee
1	Cathy (Kyashii キャシー)	American	New York (Nyūyōku ニューヨーク)	teacher
2	Eric (Erikku エリック)	French	Paris (Pari パリ)	researcher
3	Wang (Wan ワン)	Chinese	Beijing (Pekin ペキン)	working for Tōshibo
4	Your friend's name			

ex) **Kochira wa Matsuda san desu. Matsuda san wa Nihon jin desu. Chiba kara kimashita. Kaishain desu.**

こちらはまつださんです。まつださんはにほんじんです。
ちばからきました。かいしゃいんです。

1)

2)

3)

4)

Listening practice

🎧 Track1-14

Listen to the recording and find out name, nationality, hometown, and occupation. Note: not all information might be given.

	name	nationality	hometown	occupation
1				
2				
3				
4				
5				

Further practice

 Track1-15

Substitute the underlined words with the word(s) in parentheses.

1. A: Sumimasen. <u>Kōru</u> san desu ka.
   すみません。コールさんですか。
   Excuse me. Are you <u>Ms.Cole</u>?
   B: <u>Hai</u>, sō desu. はい、そうです。<u>Yes</u>, I am. /
   <u>Iie</u>, chigaimasu. いいえ、ちがいます。<u>No</u>, I'm not.

a) A: (Mr. Hosoki) B: (Yes)
b) A: (Ms. Aikawa) B: (No)
c) A: (Mr. Harada) B: (Yes)
d) A: (Ms. Suzuki) B: (No)
e) A: (Mr. Saitō) B: (Yes)

2. Hajimemashite. <u>Kobayashi</u> desu. <u>Sakura daigaku</u> no <u>gakusei</u> desu. Yoroshiku onegaishimasu.
   はじめまして。こばやしです。さくらだいがくのがくせいです。よろしくおねがいします。
   How do you do? I'm Kobayashi. I'm a student of Sakura University. Nice to meet you.

a) (Akimoto, Fujiyama University, researcher)
b) (Kishida, Hoshi Hospital, nurse)
c) (Galante, Microhard, engineer)
d) (Tanya, Honba, employee)

3. A: Doko kara kimashita ka. どこからきましたか。
   Where are you from?
   B: <u>Rondon</u> kara kimashita. ロンドンからきました。
   I'm from London.

a) (Berlin)
b) (Los Angels)
c) (Amsterdam)
d) (Okinawa)
e) (Madrid)

4. A: <u>Amerika jin</u> desu ka. アメリカじんですか。
   Are you American?
   B: Iie, <u>Igirisu jin</u> desu. いいえ、イギリスじんです。
   No, I'm British.

a) A: (Australian) B: (New Zealander)
b) A: (Chinese) B: (South Korean)
c) A: (French) B: (Canadian)
d) A: (Spanish) B: (Italian)
e) A: (Mexican) B: (Brazilian)

5. Translate into Japanese.

a) Excuse me. Are you Mr Honda?   No, I am not.
b) How do you do? I am Saitō. Nice to meet you.
c) Are you British, Ms Brown?   No, I am Singaporean.
d) Are you a teacher, Mr Aoki?   No, I am a student.
e) Miss Kawai works for a hospital.
f) Mr Nishimoto is a friend of mine.
g) Did you come from Ireland?
   No, I came from the Netherlands.

Hiragana reading Quiz 1 (Optional)

 Track1-16

This quiz is optional. You don't have to read Hiragana if your main interest is oral communication. However, it would be interesting if you learn these unique letters. So give it a try! You can find letter tables in Chapter 0.

Please write these Hiragana words in rōmaji (English letters). Then listen to the recordings.

1) あき   2) ふゆ   3) はる   4) なつ   5) くるま   6) にほん

7) しま   8) ちかてつ   9) いぬ   10) ゆき   11) とけい

12) ほん   13) かさ   14) つくえ   15) いす   16) はさみ

17) やま   18) さかな   19) にく   20) やさい   21) はな

Key Sentences

 Track1-17

These are the most important sentences in this chapter. Learn by heart!

Hajimemashite. Sumisu desu. Gōrudo ginkō de hataraite imasu. Yoroshiku onegaishimasu.

はじめまして。スミスです。ゴールドぎんこうではたらいています。よろしくおねがいします。

How do you do? I'm Smith. I work for Gold Bank. Nice to meet you.

Sumisu san wa Amerika jin desu ka.

スミスさんはアメリカじんですか。

Are you American, Ms. Smith?

Iie, Igirisu jin desu.   いいえ、イギリスじんです。

No, I'm British.

Cultural Information - Bowing (Ojigi おじぎ)

We love bowing. You might see in films or anime that Japanese people greet each other by bowing. Bowing is a part of our communication. Doing a bow is a way to show our respect for other people or even things.

There are so many ways of bowing, and it depends on the situation, so it may be confusing how to bow correctly. As a tourist, following the simple instruction below will suffice.

- When you introduce yourself, do a 30-degree bow after "**yoroshiku onegaishimasu.** よろしくおねがいします"
- When you greet someone you have already known, just doing a 15-degree bow after greetings (for example, "**ohayō gozaimasu** おはようございます") is fine.
- When you notice someone bow at you, simply bow back.

It might be a bit awkward for you to bow at first. But, like other customs, the longer you stay in Japan, the better you get used to bowing at others. Please don't worry and enjoy this new way of communication!

Congratulations! You have finished Chapter 1!

Chapter 2. Eating out

Japanese food is really popular. Many people love Japanese dishes like sushi, tempura, sashimi. Eating excellent Japanese food at a restaurant must be a highlight of your trip. Or perhaps you might try some special Japanese-style hamburgers which are available at famous global fast-food restaurants.

In this chapter, you will learn how to

- Ask what kind of food is on the menu
- Say how much food you want
- Ask for a bill

Are you hungry? Let's go and eat!

Sashimi set meal

Dialogue 1: What Is this? Koro wa nan desu ka.

🎧 Track2-1

Ms. Smith goes to a Japanese restaurant at lunchtime with Yamada san. She finds a lot of unfamiliar food names on the menu. See what happens.

Resutoran de

Omise no hito	Irasshaimase. Kochira ga menyū desu.
Yamada	Yakizakana teishoku wo onegaishimasu.
Sumisu	Ano, kore wa nan desu ka.
Omise no hito	Sashimi teishoku desu.
Sumisu	Sō desu ka. Ja, kore wo onegaishimasu.
Omise no hito	Kashikomari mashita.

レストランで

お店のひと	いらっしゃいませ。こちらがメニューです。
山田	焼き魚定食をお願いします。
スミス	あの、これはなんですか。
お店のひと	さしみ定食です。
スミス	そうですか。じゃ、これをお願いします。
お店のひと	かしこまりました。

At a restaurant

Waitress	Welcome. Here is the menu.
Yamada	The grilled fish set meal, please.
Smith	Ah, what is this?
Waitress	It is the Sashimi set meal.
Smith	I see. OK. This one, please.
Waitress	All right. (very polite expression)

Vocabulary   ☐ Deck2

resutoran restaurant   **irasshaimase** may I help you? welcome   **ga** (particle indicating subject)   **menyū** menu **yakizakana** grilled fish **teishoku** meal set (usually with rice and miso soup)   **wo** (particle indicating object) **onegaishimasu** please   **kore** this (this one)   **nan** what **sashimi**   sashimi (sliced raw fish)   **ja** well then, OK **kashikomari mashita** all right (a polite expression used by shop people)

Grammar and Expressions

🎧 Track2-2

1. Particle "ga が"

In this dialogue, the waitress says,

Kochira ga menyū desu. こちらがメニューです。

This is the menu.

"**Ga が**" is the particle that indicates the subject of the sentence.

We have already learned a similar sentence used the particle "**wa** は."

Kochira wa Kobayashi san desu.

こちらはこばやしさんです。   This is Miss. Kobayashi.

Why does the first sentence use "**ga が**" while the sentence uses "**wa** は"?

Let's see the difference between "**ga が**" and "**wa** は."

- The main difference is that "**ga** が" is a subject marker and "**wa** は" is a topic marker.
- When the subject is also the topic, "**wa** は" is used.
- The meaning of "**wa** は" is similar to the English expression, "speaking of ...." The second sentence is like this: "Speaking of this person, this is Miss Kobayashi."

"**Wa** は" and "**ga** が" are easily muddled up. But please don't worry. Any Japanese people will understand you perfectly!

2. This/ That

In this dialogue, Sumisu san asks,

Kore wa nan desu ka. これはなんですか。 What is this?

"**Nan** なん" means "what" and "**kore** これ" means "this."

The answer to this sentence is

Sashimi teishoku desu. さしみ定食です。
It is the Sashimi set meal.

In this answer, there is no "it." We don't mention the word "it" generally in Japanese, just like we dropped "I (**watashi** わたし)" in the previous chapter.

Sumisu desu. スミスです。 I'm Smith.

Now we have learned "this" is "**kore** これ," let's move on to "that."

In the Japanese language, we have two kinds of "that."
1. Far from the speaker, but near the listener **sore** それ

2. Far from both the speaker and the listener **are** あれ

Imagine that you find your friend holding some strange object in his hand. So you would like to find out what he holds. In this case, your friend is the listener, and the strange thing is in his hand, very near to him. So you use the word "**sore** それ."

Sore wa nan desu ka. それはなんですか。What is that?

His answer is

Kore wa enpitsu desu. これはえんぴつです。

This is a pencil. *****enpitsu** pencil

For him, the pencil is near to him, so he uses the word "**kore** これ." Umm, it must be a very strange-looking pencil if you need to ask what it is!

Let's look at another example. You find some strange flying object in the night sky. You ask your friend, shivering,

Are wa nan desu ka.   あれはなんですか。What is that?

Your friend will answer,

Are wa UFO (yūfō) desu.   あれは UFO です。

That is a UFO. * **yūfō** UFO

The unidentified flying object is far from both you and your friend, so you use the word "**are** あれ."

Did you get it?

3. *Ordering something in a restaurant*

In this dialogue, Ms. Smith orders her lunch like this.

Kore wo onegaishimasu. これをおねがいします。

This one, please.

"**Wo** を" is a particle that indicates a direct object.

When you would like to order something, this expression is for you.

(Something) wo onegaishimasu. ( )をおねがいします。

(Something), please.

Do you want to eat ramen noodles? Then, simply say

Rāmen wo onegaishimasu. ラーメンをおねがいします。

Ramen, please.

If you point a food name on the menu that is very close to you, then you use the word "**kore** これ."

Kore wo onegaishimasu. これをおねがいします。

This one, please.

If you find something that looks yummy on someone else's table over there, you may secretly point to that food and whisper to the waiter,

Are wo onegaishimasu.　あれをおねがいします。

That one, please.

Yes, someone else's food always looks yummy... but it's impolite to point at other people in Japan. Be careful, please!

Practice Dialogue 1

 Track2-3

Now is the time for practice! You are Sumisu san. Are you ready to order?

Omise no hito	Irasshaimase. Kochira ga menyū desu.
Yamada	Yakizakana teishoku wo onegaishimasu.
Sumisu	(ask "Ah, what is this?")
Omise no hito	Sashimi teishoku desu.
Sumisu	(say "I see." and order it)
Omise no hito	Kashikomari mashita.

You managed to order your lunch! Hurray!

Would you like to act "omise no hito"? I don't think you will have much opportunity to be a waiter or waitress in Japan, but to put yourself into someone's shoes is always a better way to understand a situation, isn't it? So let's try!

Omise no hito	(greet your customer and say, "here is the menu")
Yamada	Yakizakana teishoku wo onegaishimasu.
Sumisu	Ano, kore wa nan desu ka.
Omise no hito	(answer "it's Sashimi set meal")
Sumisu	Sō desu ka. Ja, kore wo onegaishimasu.
Omise no hito	(say "all right" in a polite manner)

Well done!

Dialogue 2: The bill, please. Okaikei wo onegaishimasu.

 Track2-4

Now Ms. Smith and Yamada san start eating. They seem to be enjoying their meal.

Sumisu	Itadakimasu.
Yamada	Itadakimasu.
Sumisu	Oishii desu ne.
Yamada	Sō desu ne.
Sumisu	Gochisōsama deshita.
Yamada	Gochisōsama deshita.
	Sumimasen. Okaikei wo onegaishimasu.
Omise no hito	Shōshō omachi kudasai. ...
	Okaikei wa kochira desu. Reji made omochi kudasai.
Reji de	
Yamada	Kore wo onegaishimasu.
Reji no hito	Goissho desu ka.
Yamada	Iie, betsubetsu de onegaishimasu.
Reji no hito	Kyūhyaku hachijū en to sen nijū en desu. Kochira ga reshiito desu. Arigatō gozaimashita.

スミス　　　　　いただきます。

山田　　　　　　いただきます。

スミス　　　　　おいしいですね。

山田　　　　　　そうですね。

スミス　　　　　ごちそうさまでした。

山田　　　　　　ごちそうさまでした。

　　　　　　　　すみません。お会計をお願いしま

お店のひと	す。 少々お待ちください。... お会計はこちらです。レジまでおもちください。

レジで

山田さん	これをお願いします。
レジのひと	ごいっしょですか。
山田さん	いいえ、べつべつでお願いします。
レジのひと	９８０円と１０２０円です。こちらがレシートです。ありがとうございました。

Smith	Itadakimasu.
Yamada	Itadakimasu.
Smith	It is delicious.
Yamada	Yes indeed.
Smith	Gochisōsama deshita.
Yamada	Gochisōsama deshita.
	Excuse me. The bill, please.
Waitress	Please wait a moment.
	Here is the bill. Please take it to the cash register.

At the cash register

Yamada	(I'd like to pay) this, please.
Cashier	Would you like to pay together?
Yamada	No, separately, please.
Cashier	980 yen and 1020 yen. (She receives money from them.) These are the receipts. Thank you very much.

Vocabulary   ☐ Deck2

itadakimasu (said before eating a meal)   **oishii** delicious
ne   isn't it? right?   (particle)   **sō desu ne**   yes indeed
gochisōsama deshita (said after eating a meal)   **okaikei**
bill **shōshō** a little   **omachi kudasai** please wait (polite)
reji cash desk   **made** to, as far as (particle)   **omochi
kudasai** please take   **goissho** together (polite)
betsubetsu separately   **to** and **en** Japanese yen   **reshiito**
receipt   **arigatō gozaimashita** Thank you (past tense)

Grammar and Expressions

🎧 Track2-5

1. Set phrases at mealtimes

When we start eating, we say:

Itadakimasu. いただきます。

And when we finish eating, we say

Gochisōsama deshita.　ごちそうさまでした。

"**Itadakimasu** いただきます" shows our gratitude for the
food and for the people who prepared the meal.
"**Gochisōsama deshita** ごちそうさまでした" also express
our appreciation for the hard work to prepare such a nice
meal. While we are saying these set phrases, we usually put
our hands together in front of our chest in a prayer position
and make a bow.

2. Giving responses during conversation

In this dialogue, when Ms. Smith says, "**Oishii desu ne** おいし

いですね," Yamada san says,

Sō desu ne. そうですね。   Yes, indeed.

(when you agree with what someone's saying)

Japanese people love to give responses, we call them "**aizuchi** あいづち," and frequently use them during conversation. Here are some other examples.

Hē へえ or **Un** うん are similar to "Uh-huh."

Ii desu ne. いいですね。Sounds good.

Sō desu ka. そうですか。Oh, really?

(when you hear the new information)

And you should nod your head frequently to let him or her know you are listening!

Practice Dialogue 2

🎧 Track2-6

Now it's time to eat! Be Ms. Smith and speak aloud the meal time set phrases with the prayer-like action!

Sumisu	(Say the set phrase before eating)
Yamada	Itadakimasu.
Sumisu	(Say "it's delicious")
Yamada	Sō desu ne.
Sumisu	(Say the greeting after the meal)
Yamada	Gochisōsama deshita.

Did you put your hands together in front of your chest and

bow? Well done! Everybody around the table must be impressed!

After you enjoy your meal at the good restaurant, now is the time for payment. Let's practice Yamada san's part.

Yamada	(Say "excuse me" and ask the bill)
Omise no hito	Shōshō omachi kudasai. ...
	Okaikei wa kochira desu. Reji made omochi kudasai.

Reji de

Yamada	(Hand the bill to the cashier and say please)
Reji no hito	Goissho desu ka.
Yamada	(Say "no, separately, please.")
Reji no hito	Kyūhyaku hachijū en to senniju en desu. Kochira ga reshiito desu. Arigatō gozaimashita.

Wonderful!

Dialogue 3: Two hamburgers, please. Hanbāgā wo futatsu onegaishimasu.

🎧 Track2-7

Ms. Smith loves Japanese food, but sometimes she is in the mood to go to a fast-food shop. The way you order is slightly different. Let's see what happens.

Fāsuto fūdo de

Omise no hito	Irasshaimase. Okimari desu ka.
Sumisu	Hanbāgā wo futatsu onegaishimasu.
Omise no hito	Kashikomari mashita. Onomimono wa ikaga desu ka.
Sumisu	Kōhii wo onegaishimasu.
Omise no hito	Kashikomari mashita. Tennai de omeshiagari desu ka.
Sumis	Iie, mochikaeri de onegaishimasu.
Omise no hito	Kashikomari mashita. Gohyaku sanjū en desu.
Sumisu	Hai.
Omise no hito	Nana jū en no otsuri desu. Arigatō gozaimashita.

ファーストフードで

お店のひと	いらっしゃいませ。おきまりですか。
スミス	ハンバーガーをふたつお願いします。
お店のひと	かしこまりました。お飲み物はいかがですか。
スミス	コーヒーをお願いします。
お店のひと	かしこまりました。店内でおめしあがりですか。

スミス	いいえ、もちかえりでお願いします。
お店のひと	かしこまりました。５３０円です。
スミス	はい。
お店のひと	７０円のおつりです。ありがとうございました。

At a fast food shop

Shop attendant	Welcome. Have you decided on your order?
Smith	Two hamburgers, please.
Shop attendant	All right. How about drinks?
Smith	Coffee, please.
Shop attendant	All right. Is that to eat in?
Smith	No, takeaway, please.
Shop attendant	All right. That's 530 yen.
Smith	Yes.
Shop attendant	Here is your 70 yen change. Thank you very much.

Vocabulary ⬜ Deck2

fāsuto fūdo fast food shop **okimari desu ka** have you decided on your order?   **futatsu** two (special number for counting things, see next page) **kashikomari mashita** all right (a polite expression used by shop staff only) **onomimono** (something to) drink **ikaga desu ka** how about ... ? (polite) **kōhii** coffee   **tennai** inside a shop   **de** at (particle) **omeshiagari** to eat (polite)   **mochikaeri** takeaway **de** by (particle)   **otsuri** change

Grammar and Expressions

 Track2-8

1. General Counters

Japanese doesn't distinguish between singular and plural. "**Ringo** りんご (apple)" is always "**ringo** りんご," regardless of whether it's 1 or 1,000s. This is good news, isn't it? However, the bad news is, if you would like to mention how many things you need or buy, you should use the special words for counting things called "counters."

So what are counters? They show quantity, but they also express a certain quality about objects being counted. For example, there is a counter for long objects like bottles (-**hon** ほん), for thin, flat objects like a piece of paper or shirt (-**mai** まい), for people (-**nin** にん), for machines and vehicles (-**dai** だい) and so on. You should use an appropriate counter for the things you count.

Sounds complicated?

Yes, I'm afraid so, but don't worry. I would like to show you a shortcut named "general counters."

General counters can be used to count almost anything. The only restrictions you should know are that you can use them **up to 10** and you **cannot use them to count people or animals**!

1	**hitotsu**	ひとつ
2	**futatsu**	ふたつ
3	**mittsu**	みっつ
4	**yottsu**	よっつ

5	**itsutsu**	いつつ
6	**muttsu**	むっつ
7	**nanatsu**	ななつ
8	**yattsu**	やっつ
9	**kokonotsu**	ここのつ
10	**tō**	とお

Now you have got the general counters, how do you use them?

Imagine you would like to order 2 hamburgers. You should tell the shop attendant how many you want. Do you remember how to say the counter for "2"? Yes, it's "**futatsu** ふたつ"!

Hanbāgā wo <u>futatsu</u> onegaishimasu.

ハンバーガーをふたつおねがいします。

Two hamburgers, please.

(Noun) wo (counter) onegaishimasu.

(Noun) を (counter)おねがいします。

(Number)(Noun), please.

Could you say "3 hamburgers, please"?

Yes, "**Hanbāgā wo <u>mittsu</u> onegaishimasu.** ハンバーガーを みっつおねがいします。"

Well Done!

Practice Dialogue 3

 Track2-9

Let's begin ordering. You are Sumisu san now.

Omise no hito	Irasshaimase. Okimari deshō ka.
Sumisu	(Say "two hamburgers, please")
Omise no hito	Kashikomari mashita. Onomimono wa ikaga desu ka.
Sumisu	(Say "Coffee, please.")
Omise no hito	Kashikomari mashita. Tennai de omeshiagari desu ka.
Sumisu	(Say "No, takeaway, please.")
Omise no hito	Kashikomari mashita. Gohyaku sanjū en desu.
Sumisu	(Say "Yes" and give 600yen)
Omise no hito	Nana jū en no otsuri desu. Arigatō gozaimashita.

Great!
Would you like to be "omise no hito"? Why not? Let's try!

Omise no hito	(Say "Welcome. Have you decided your order?")
Sumisu	Hanbāgā wo futatsu onegaishimasu.
Omise no hito	(Say "All right. How about drinks?")
Sumisu	Kōhii wo onegaishimasu.
Omise no hito	(Say "All right. Will you eat at the shop?")
Sumisu	Iie, mochikaeri de onegaishimasu.
Omise no hito	(Say "All right. 530 yen.")
Sumisu	Hai.
Omise no hito	(Say "Here is your 70 yen change. Thank you very much.")

What excellent customer service! Good job!

Related Vocabulary 🔲 Deck2

Drink and Food

🎧 Track2-10

To order at the restaurant or café, you need to know some food vocabulary. Here is the list.

drinks	**nomimono** のみもの
coffee	**kōhii** コーヒー
tea	**kōcha** こうちゃ
green tea	**ocha** おちゃ
juice	**jūsu** ジュース
water	**mizu** みず
milk	**miruku / gyūnū** ミルク / ぎゅうにゅう
beer	**biiru** ビール
wine	**wain** ワイン
sake	**osake** おさけ
foods	**tabemono** たべもの
bread	**pan** パン
rice	**gohan** ごはん
soup	**sūpu** スープ
miso soup	**misoshiru** みそしる
sandwich	**sandoicchi** サンドイッチ
salad	**sarada** サラダ
hotdog	**hotto doggu** ホットドッグ
hamburger	**hanbāgā** ハンバーガー
pizza	**piza** ピザ

spaghetti	**supagetti** スパゲッティ
sushi	**sushi** すし
curry and rice	**karēraisu** カレーライス
sashimi	**sashimi** さしみ
grilled fish	**yakizakana** やきざかな
stewed fish	**nizakana** にざかな
grilled meat	**yakiniku** やきにく
tempura	**tempura** てんぷら
ramen noodles	**rāmen** ラーメン
udon noodles	**udon** うどん
soba noodles	**soba** そば
deserts	**dezāto** デザート
cake	**kēki** ケーキ
chocolate	**chokorēto** チョコレート
ice cream	**aisukuriimu** アイスクリーム
dish, cuisine	**ryōri** りょうり
(country)dish-	**-ryōri** りょうり
Japanese cuisine	**Nihon ryōri** にほんりょうり
French cuisine	**Furansu ryōri** フランスりょうり
Italian cuisine	**Itaria ryōri** イタリアりょうり
fish	**sakana** さかな
salmon	**sake** さけ
tuna	**maguro** まぐろ
meat	**niku** にく
beef	**gyūniku** ぎゅうにく
pork	**butaniku** ぶたにく

chicken	**toriniku** とりにく
eggs	**tamago** たまご

vegetables	**yasai** やさい
potato	**jagaimo** じゃがいも
carrot	**ninjin** にんじん
onion	**tamanegi** たまねぎ
sweet potato	**satsumaimo** さつまいも
pumpkin	**kabocha** かぼちゃ
tomato	**tomato** トマト

fruits	**kudamono** くだもの
apple	**ringo** りんご
orange	**mikan** みかん
pear	**nashi** なし
grapes	**budō** ぶどう
banana	**banana** バナナ
strawberry	**ichigo** いちご

Phew! We can add more, but let's move on to the next topic.

Numbers

🎧 Track2-11

Numbers are useful. Numbers are essential. But many people think memorizing numbers is difficult. Please don't worry. To count numbers in Japanese is not as difficult as you think. Let's start counting the basic numbers!

0	**zero / rei** ゼロ・れい
1	**ichi** いち

2   **ni** に
3   **san** さん
4   **yon / shi** よん・し
5   **go** ご
6   **roku** ろく
7   **nana / shichi** なな・しち
8   **hachi** はち
9   **kyū / ku** きゅう・く
10   **jū** じゅう

As you can see, 4, 7, and 9 have two names. It would help if you memorized both because each of them is used in a particular situation. I will explain it to you in the later chapters.

Then, all teens...

11   **jū ichi** じゅういち
12   **jū ni** じゅうに
13   **jū san** じゅうさん
14   **jū yon / jū shi** じゅうよん・じゅうし
15   **jū go** じゅうご
16   **jū roku** じゅうろく
17   **jū nana / jū shichi** じゅうなな・じゅうしち

18   **jū hachi** じゅうはち
19   **jū kyū / jū ku** じゅうきゅう・じゅうく

Now you can see how easy Japanese numbers are. 11 is 10 and 1. 12 is 10 and 2, and so on. Logical!

How do you say 20? 2 and 10 are 20! Super simple! Can you guess how to say 25? Yes, 2 and 10 and 5, and voila! 25!

20	**nijū** にじゅう	
21	**nijū ichi** にじゅういち	
22	**nijū ni** にじゅうに	
23	**nijū san** にじゅうさん	
24	**nijū yon / nijū shi** にじゅうよん・にじゅうし	
25	**nijū go** にじゅうご	
26	**nijū roku** にじゅうろく	
27	**nijū nana / nijū shichi** にじゅうなな・にじゅうしち	
28	**nijū hachi** にじゅうはち	
29	**nijū kyū / nijū ku** にじゅうきゅう・にじゅうく	
30	**sanjū** さんじゅう	

Now we can go up to 100!

40	**yonjū** よんじゅう
50	**gojū** ごじゅう
60	**rokujū** ろくじゅう
70	**nanajū** ななじゅう
80	**hachijū** はちじゅう
90	**kyūjū** きゅうじゅう
100	**hyaku** ひゃく

Are you ready to go beyond 100 to 1000?

100	**hyaku** ひゃく
200	**nihyaku** にひゃく

300 **sanbyaku** さんびゃく

400 **yonhyaku** よんひゃく

500 **gohyaku** ごひゃく

600 **roppyaku** ろっぴゃく

700 **nanahyaku** ななひゃく

800 **happyaku** はっぴゃく

900 **kyūhyaku** きゅうひゃく

1,000 **sen** せん

Let's revise a bit. Can you say "132" in Japanese? Yes, "**hyaku sanjū ni** ひゃくさんじゅうに"! 764? Yes, "**nanahyaku rokujū yon** ななひゃくろくじゅうよん"! Wonderful!

From 1000 to 10,000 is...

1,000 **sen** せん

2,000 **nisen** にせん

3,000 **sanzen** さんぜん

4,000 **yonsen** よんせん

5,000 **gosen** ごせん

6,000 **rokusen** ろくせん

7,000 **nanasen** ななせん

8,000 **hassen** はっせん

9,000 **kyūsen** きゅうせん

10,000 **ichiman** いちまん

10,000 is a special number in the Japanese counting system. We don't count it as "10 and thousand" like English. We use the particular unit called "**man** まん." 10,000 is called as "1 and **man**". I know it is a bit confusing, but "**man**" is not so bad once you get used to it. Let's see.

10,000   **ichiman** いちまん

20,000   **niman** にまん

30,000   **sanman** さんまん

40,000   **yonman** よんまん

50,000   **goman** ごまん

60,000   **rokuman** ろくまん

70,000   **nanaman** ななまん

80,000   **hachiman** はちまん

90,000   **kyūman** きゅうまん

100,000   **jūman** じゅうまん

As you can see, "**man** まん" is really easy to count. It won't change, unlike "**hyaku** ひゃく" or "**sen** せん." You just say "10 and **man** まん", "25 and **man** まん", "999 and **man** まん" and "8257 and **man** まん". Isn't it great?

100,000   **jūman** じゅうまん

250,000   **nijūgoman** にじゅうごまん

9,990,000   **kyūhyaku kyūjū kyū man**
                        きゅうひゃくきゅうじゅうきゅうまん

82,570,000   **hassen nihyaku gojū nana man**
                        はっせんにひゃくごじゅうななまん

Would you like to know more big numbers like million, billion, or trillion? You may buy a local company or a huge penthouse. In this case, these numbers are really useful!

100,000	**jūman** じゅうまん
1,000,000	**hyakuman** ひゃくまん
10,000,000	**senman** せんまん
100,000,000	**ichioku** いちおく
1,000,000,000	**jūoku** じゅうおく
10,000,000,000	**hyakuoku** ひゃくおく
100,000,000,000	**senoku** せんおく
1,000,000,000,000	**itchō** いっちょう

Speaking practice

 Track2-12

Are you hungry? Let's order your meal!

1) Curry and rice, please.
2) Beer, please.
3) Pizza and coffee, please.
4) Two ice cream, please.
5) 3 cups of tea, please.
6) 5 hot dogs, please.
7) 6 grilled fish and four grilled portions of meat, please.

Listening practice

 Track2-13

1. Listen to the recordings and find out what the person orders.

a)

b)

c)

d)

2. Listen and find out how much it is.

a)

b)

c)

d)

Further practice

🎧 Track2-14

Substitute the underlined word(s) with the word(s) in parentheses.

1. ex.) <u>Kore</u> wa nan desu ka. <u>これ</u>はなんですか。
What is <u>this</u>?

a) (That (far from the speaker, but near the listener))
b) (That (far from both the speaker and the listener))

2. ex.) <u>Yonhyaku</u> en desu. <u>よんひゃく</u>えんです。
It's <u>400</u> yen.

a) (800 yen)
b) (2,000 yen)
c) (7,100 yen)
d) (9,999 yen)
e) (35,768 yen)
f) (148,600 yen)

3. ex.) <u>Hanbāgā wo futatsu</u> onegaishimasu.
<u>ハンバーガーをふたつ</u>おねがいします。

<u>2 hamburgers</u>, please.

a) (3 sandwiches)
b) (5 eggs)
c) (6 apples)
d) (4 salads)
e) (7 cakes)

4. Translate into Japanese

a) A: What is this?
    B: This is soba noodles.
    A: I see. Well then, this one, please.
b) (Set phrase before eating)
c) (Set phrase after eating)
d) It is delicious, isn't it?
e) Excuse me. Bill, please.
f) A: Four breads, please.   B: 470 yen.
g) A: Cake and tea, please. B: 750 yen.
h) How do you do. I am Shirota. I am a student of Hakone
    university. Nice to meet you.

Hiragana Reading Quiz 2 (Optional)

🎧 Track2-15

In this reading quiz, you can find some long vowels and small
"**tsu** つ". If you are not sure how to read long vowels and
small "**tsu** つ" or any other hiragana, please feel free to go
back to chapter 0 and check them.

1)おかあさん 2)おとうさん　3) おねえさん　4)おにいさん
5) ゆうき　6) ぼうし　7) きって　8) ざっし 9) しゃしん
10)きゅうきゅうしゃ　11)しょうぼうしゃ　12)こうちゃ
13)びょういん　14) じゃがいも　15)ぎゅうにゅう

16) ひゃくえん 17) じゅうえん　18) りょこう 19) おべん
とう　20) とうきょう　21) きょうと

Key sentences

🎧 Track2-16

Kore wa nan desu ka. これはなんですか。What is this?

Okaikei wo onegaishimasu.

おかいけいをおねがいします。The bill, please.

Hanbāgā wo futatsu onegaishimasu.

ハンバーガーをふたつおねがいします。

Two hamburgers, please.

Cultural Information – Table manners

It would be exciting to go to authentic Japanese restaurants. Here are some tips to behave well at the Japanese table.

- Always say "**Itadakimasu** いただきます" and "**Gochisōsama deshita** ごちそうさまでした" at mealtimes. These set phrases are really important. If you can, put your hands together in front of your chest in a prayer position and make a bow.

- When rice is served in a small rice bowl called "**ochawan** おちゃわん," please pick it up, raise it to your chest and eat. If soup is in a small soup bowl called "**owan** おわん," pick it up and raise it to your chest when you eat the ingredients, or raise it to your lips and drink directly.

- When you drink beer or other alcoholic drinks, you should wait until all the glasses are filled and someone gives a toast, "**kanpai** かんぱい." If we have bottles of wine or beer at the table, we usually serve each other rather than pour our glasses by ourselves.

- There is no tipping in Japan. If you would like to show your gratitude to a waitress or a shop clerk, please give them a big smile, say "**Arigatō gozaimasu** ありがとうございます" and give a bow.

Happy eating!

Chapter 3. Shopping

Shopping is fun, especially in a different part of the world! In Japan, you may find some old Japanese antiques in a flea market or get your favorite anime figure in Akihabara. Even just buying something like milk or bread at a supermarket can be an exciting experience!

In this chapter, you will learn how to

- Ask where are the products you want to buy.
- Ask how much it is.
- Ask permission to try on clothes.

Are you ready? Grab your purse, and let's go shopping!

A cashier at a Japanese supermarket

Dialogue 1: Where is milk? Gyūnyū wa doko desu ka.

🎧 Track3-1

Ms. Smith goes to a supermarket nearby to buy a carton of milk. It looks a bit difficult for her to find where the milk is. Let's see what happens.

Sūpā de

Omise no hito	Irasshaimase.
Sumisu	Sumimasen. Gyūnyū wa doko desu ka.
Omise no hito	Gyūnyū wa asoko desu.
Sumisu	Etto, doko desu ka.
Omise no hito	Asoko ni sakana uriba ga arimasu ne. Gyūnyū wa sakana uriba no tonari desu.
Sumisu	Wakarimashita. Arigatō gozaimasu.

スーパーで

お店のひと	いらっしゃいませ。
スミス	すみません。牛乳はどこですか。
お店のひと	牛乳はあそこです。
スミス	えっと、どこですか。
お店のひと	あそこに魚売り場がありますね。牛乳は魚売り場のとなりです。
スミス	わかりました。ありがとうございます。

At a supermarket

Shop clerk	Welcome.
Smith	Excuse me. Where is milk?
Shop clerk	Milk is over there.
Smith	Uh, where is it?
Shop clerk	There is a fish section over there. The milk is next to the fish section.

Smith   I see. Thank you.

Vocabulary   Deck3

sūpā supermarket **gyūnyū** milk **doko** where   **asoko** over there   **etto** uh   **sakana** fish **uriba** section (selling area in a store)   **arimasu** be, exist, there is/are (for non-living)   cf. **imasu** (for living)) **tonari** next to **wakarimashita** (Lit.)I understood

---

Grammar and Expressions

 Track3-2
1. Here/There/Where

In this Dialogue, Ms. Smith asks,

Gyūnyū wa doko desu ka. ぎゅうにゅうはどこですか。

Where is the milk?

"**Doko** どこ" means "where."

Omise no hito answers:

Gyūnyū wa asoko desu. ぎゅうにゅうはあそこです。

Milk is over there.

"**Asoko** あそこ" means "over there." Do you remember Japanese has two kinds of "that"? Yes, "**sore** それ" and "**are** あれ." "**Sore** それ" means far from the speaker, but near the listener. "**Are** あれ" means far from both the speaker and the listener. "There" is the same.
 If you would like to indicate the place far from you, but near the listener, you use "**soko** そこ."
If you mean the place far from both you and the listener, you use "**asoko** あそこ."

Then, if you want to mention "here"? Can you guess? Yes, **"koko こ こ."**

Imagine you would like to buy bread. You ask a shop clerk:

Pan wa doko desu ka. パンはどこ ですか。 Where is bread?

If bread is near the shop clerk, she will answer:

Pan wa koko desu. パンはここ です。 Bread is here.

If bread is a bit far from her, but near you, she will say:

Pan wa soko desu. パンはそこ です。 Bread is there.

If bread is over there, she will answer:

Pan wa asoko desu.   パンはあそこ です。

Bread is over there.

If the shop clerk would like to use slightly politer words than **koko**, **soko**, **asoko**, she will use "**kochira こ ち ら,**" "**sochira そ ち ら**" and "**achira あ ち ら。**" The politer word for **doko** is "**dochira ど ち ら**".

(Noun) wa doko / dochira desu ka. Where is (noun)?

(Noun) wa koko / kochira desu. (Noun) is here.

(Noun) wa soko / sochira desu. (Noun) is there (near to the listener)

(Noun) wa asoko / achira desu. (Noun) is over there. (far from the speaker and the listener)

Did you get it?

2. There is/are

In the dialogue, the shop clerk says,

Asoko ni sakana uriba ga arimasu ne.

あそこにさかなうりばがありますね。

> There is a fish section over there.

It's a bit of a long sentence so let's break it down.

The central part of this sentence is

Sakana uriba ga arimasu. さかなうりばがあります。

> There is a fish section.

"**Arimasu** あります" means "there is" or "exist."

To indicate the place, "**asoko ni** あそこに (over there)" is added.

Asoko ni sakana uriba ga arimasu.

あそこにさかなうりばがあります。

> There is a fish section over there.

Then at the end of the sentence, "**ne** ね" is added.

"**Ne** ね" is a particle. It is a gentle request for confirmation from a listener. In this dialogue, the shop clerk would like to confirm whether Ms. Smith can see the fish counter or not. That is why she uses "**ne** ね."

Asoko ni sakana uriba ga arimasu ne.

あそこにさかなうりばがありますね。

> There is a fish counter over there, isn't there?

Let's go a bit further. If you would like to mention people or animals, you should use "**imasu** います," instead of "**arimasu** あります."

Asoko ni Yamada san ga imasu.

あそこにやまださんがいます。 Yamada san is over there.

3. Positions

In this dialogue, you hear "**tonari** となり" which means "next to."
Let's check the words which indicate positions.

front	**mae** まえ
back	**ushiro** うしろ
next to	**tonari** となり
right	**migi** みぎ
left	**hidari** ひだり
top, above	**ue** うえ
under, below, bottom	**shita** した
inside, middle	**naka** なか
near, in the vicinity	**chikaku** ちかく

Let's check how to use these position words.

(Something/somebody) wa (noun) no (position) desu.

(Something/somebody)は (noun) の (position) です。

(something/someone) is (position) (noun).

Gyūnyū wa sakana uriba no tonari desu.

ぎゅうにゅうはさかなうりばのとなりです。

The Milk is next to the fish section.

If you use the position words with "**imasu/arimasu,**" you should put "**ni** に." "**ni** に" is a particle that indicates the place.

(Something/somebody) wa (noun) no (position) ni arimasu/imasu.

(Something/somebody)は(noun)の(position)にあります /

います。

(Something/somebody) is (position) (noun).

Gyūnyū wa sakana uriba no tonari <u>ni</u> arimasu.

ぎゅうにゅうはさかなうりばのとなり<u>に</u>あります。

The Milk is next to the fish section.

Practice Dialogue 1

 Track3-3

Let's practice Dialogue1! First, you play Sumisu san's part.

Omise no hito	Irasshaimase.
Sumisu	(Say "Excuse me. Where is milk?")
Omise no hito	Gyūnyū wa asoko desu.
Sumisu	(Say "where is it?")
Omise no hito	Asoko ni sakana uriba ga arimasu ne. Gyūnyū wa sakana uriba no tonari desu.
Sumisu	(Say "I understand. Thank you.")

Well done! Then, let's try "omise no hito".

Omise no hito	(Welcome your customer)
Sumisu	Sumimasen. Gyūnyū wa doko desu ka.
Omise no hito	(Say "The milk is over there.")
Sumisu	Etto, doko desu ka.
Omise no hito	(Say "There is a fish section over there, isn't there? The milk is next to fish section.")
Sumisu	Wakarimashita. Arigatō gozaimasu.

Great!

Dialogue 2: I would like to buy a skirt. Sukāto wo kaitain desu ga.

 Track3-4

Sumisu san would like to buy a new skirt, so she goes to a department store. She cannot read the floor guide, so she asks a shop clerk.

Depāto de

Sumisu	Sumimasen. Sukāto wo kaitain desu ga.
Omise no hito	Sukāto wa sangai ni gozaimasu.
Sumisu	Arigatō gozaimasu.

デパートで

スミス	すみません。スカートを 買_かいたいん ですが。
お店のひと	スカートは 3階_{さんがい}にございます。
スミスさん	ありがとうございます。

At a department store

Smith	Excuse me. I would like to buy a skirt.
Shop clerk	Skirts are on the 3rd floor.
Smith	Thank you.

Vocabulary Deck3

depāto department store **sukāto** skirt   **kaitain desu ga** I would like to buy   **sangai** the 3rd floor **–kai** (counters for floors in a building)   **gozaimasu** there is (politer expression of "arimasu")

Grammar and Expressions

 Track3-5

1. *I would like to buy (something)*

In this dialogue, Ms. Smith mentions:

Sukāto wo kaitain desu ga. スカートをかいたいんですが。
I would like to buy a skirt.

"**Kaitain desu ga**" means that "I want to buy," but it hints that "I need some help. Could you help me?"

If you just mention "I want to buy a skirt," the sentence should be like this:

Sukāto wo kaitai desu. スカートをかいたいです。

As a tourist, you likely need some help from a shop clerk when you want to buy something. So "**kaitain desu ga**" is really useful.
For example, if you would like to buy a T-shirt, you simply say:

Tshatsu wo kaitain desu ga. Tシャツをかいたいんですが。
I would like to buy a T-shirt.

Then, a shop clerk will give you some suggestions.

If you would like to buy two apples, you need to use a counter like this:

Ringo wo futatsu kaitain desu ga.
りんごをふたつかいたいんですが。
I would like to buy two apples.

(Something) wo (counter) kitain desu ga.

(Something) を(counter)かいたいんですが。

> I want to buy (counter) (something).

2. Counter for building floor "kai かい（階）"

In this dialogue, the shop clerk says,

Sukāto wa sangai ni gozaimasu.

スカートはさんがいにございます。

> The skirts are on the 3rd floor.

If you would like to count floors in a building, you use the counter "**kai** かい."

The primary usage of counters is that you link numbers and counter suffixes together. Would you please bear in mind that "kai かい" counter is a little tricky? You cannot simply connect them. There are some exceptional pronunciations.

Here is the list. I've underlined the tricky parts for you. I've also included the kanji version because you may see them on an actual floor guide in a Japanese department store. Before the "階**(kai)**" counter, we usually use kanji numerals, too.

We count the floors in an American way. There is no ground floor, but the first floor.

1st floor	**ikkai** いっかい	一階
2nd floor	**nikai** にかい	二階
3rd floor	**sangai** さんがい	三階
4th floor	**yonkai** よんかい	四階

5th floor	**gokai** ごかい	五階
6th floor	**ro<u>kk</u>ai** ろっかい	六階
7th floor	**nanakai** ななかい	七階
8th floor	**ha<u>kk</u>ai** はっかい	八階
9th floor	**kyūkai** きゅうかい	九階
10th floor	**jukkai** じゅっかい	十階

Basement 1st floor

chika i<u>kk</u>ai ちかいっかい　地下一階

which floor　**nangai** なんがい　　何階

If you would like to ask, "Which floor are shirts on?" you say,

Shatsu wa nangai ni arimasu ka.
シャツはなんがいにありますか。
or
Shatsu wa nangai desu ka.
シャツはなんがいですか。

If a shop clerk answers "**gokai ni arimasu.** ごかいにあります" or "**gokai desu** ごかいです," it means the 5th floor. Please say "**Arigatō gozaimasu** ありがとうございます" with a smile, give a bow, and go to the 5th floor.

Practice Dialogue 2

 Track3-6

Let's practice Sumisu san's part!

Sumisu	(Say "Excuse me. I would like to buy a skirt".)
Omise no hito	Sukāto wa sangai ni gozaimasu.
Sumisu	(Thank her)

Great!

I think you can guess what happens next. Yes, play an "omise no hito" role! Please remember that omise no hito uses politer expressions than the customer. Let's start.

Sumisu	Sumimasen. Sukāto wo kaitain desu ga.
Omise no hito	(Say "Skirts are on the 3rd floor.")
Sumisu	Arigatō gozaimasu.

Super job!

Dialogue 3. How much is it? Ikura desu ka.

🎧 Track3-7

Ms. Smith goes up to the 3rd floor. She finds a skirt section and speaks to a shop clerk.

Sangai

Sumisu	Sumimasen. Kore wa ikura desu ka.
Omise no hito	15,000 (ichiman gosen) en desu.
Sumisu	Sō desu ka. Chotto takai desu. Mō sukoshi yasui no wa arimasuka.
Omise no hito	Kochira wa ikaga desu ka. 10,000 (ichiman) en desu.
Sumisu	Ii desu ne. Demo chotto chiisai desu. Jūichigō wa arimasu ka.
Omise no hito	Hai. Sukoshi omachi kudasai. Kochira desu.
Sumisu	Shichaku shite mo ii desu ka.
Omise no hito	Hai. Shichaku shitsu wa achira desu.
Sumisu	Arigatō gozaimasu.

３階

スミスさん	すみません。これはいくらですか。
お店のひと	１５，０００円です。
スミスさん	そうですか。ちょっと高いです。もうすこし安いのはありますか。
お店のひと	こちらはいかがですか。１０，０００円です。
スミスさん	いいですね。でもちょっと小さいです。１１号はありますか。
お店のひと	はい。すこしお待ちください。

こちらです。

スミスさん	試着してもいいですか。
お店のひと	はい。試着室はあちらです。
スミスさん	ありがとうございます。

3rd floor

Smith	Excuse me. How much is this?
Shop clerk	15,000 yen.
Smith	I see. It is a bit expensive. Is there (Do you have) a bit cheaper one?
Shop clerk	How about this? It is 10,000 yen.
Smith	That sounds good. But it is a bit small. (Do you have) size 11?
Shop clerk	Yes. Wait a moment. Here it is.
Smith	May I try it on?
Shop clerk	Yes. The fitting room is over there.
Smith	Thank you very much.

Vocabulary   Deck3

ikura how much   **chotto / sukoshi** a bit, a little
takai expensive   **mō sukoshi** a bit more
yasui inexpensive, cheap   **no** one   **ii desu ne** sounds good
demo but   **chiisai** small   **gō** (counters for clothes size)
shichaku shite mo ii desu ka May I try it on?
cf. **shichaku shimasu** try on   **shichaku shitsu** fitting room
achira over there (polite)

Grammar and Expressions

🎧 Track3-8

1. How much?

When you buy something, you need to know the price.

Ikura desu ka. いくらですか。   How much?

If you would like to ask more precisely, you can say;

(Noun) wa ikura desu ka. (Noun)はいくらですか。

How much is (noun)?

In this dialogue, Ms. Smith asks a shop clerk:

Sukāto wa ikura desu ka. スカートはいくらですか。

How much is the skirt?

And she answers,

15,000 (ichiman gosen) en desu.

いちまんごせんえんです。   It is 15,000 yen

To ask how much it is, you should know the numbers. Please revise the "Enrich Your Vocabulary" section in Chapter2!

2. Counters for clothes sizes "gō" ごう (号)

If you would like to buy some clothes in Japan, you need to know your size. Here is the size chart for women's clothes in Japan. For clothes size, we usually use Arabic numerals.

size7	**nanagō**	ななごう　7 号
size9	**kyūgō**	きゅうごう　9 号
size11	**jūichigō**	じゅういちごう　11 号

| size13 | **jūsangō** | じゅうさんごう | 13号 |
| size15 | **jūgogō** | じゅうごごう | 15号 |

If you would like to ask the size, you say;

Kore wa nangō desu ka. これはなんごうですか。

What size is it?

If it is size 9, the answer is

Kyūgō desu. きゅうごうです。It is size 9.

Would you like to know your Japanese size? Here is the women's clothes size table.

Japan	7	9	11	13	15
US	2	4-6	8-10	12-14	16-18
UK	6	8	10	12	14
Europa	36	38	40	42	44

We also use S, M, L sizes, which are used for most men's clothes. Japanese size M may be smaller than your country's size M, though.

3. Adjectives

In this dialogue, Ms. Smith says,

Chotto takai desu. ちょっとたかいです。

It's a bit expensive.

"**Takai** たかい" means expensive. It's an adjective. Let's check some other adjectives.

expensive	**takai**	たかい
cheap, inexpensive	**yasui**	やすい
big	**ōkii**	おおきい

small	**chiisai** ちいさい
old	**furui** ふるい
	(You cannot use it for living things.)
new	**atarashii** あたらしい
heavy	**omoi** おもい
light	**karui** かるい

"**Chotto** ちょっと" and "**sukoshi** すこし" mean "a bit".

Chotto omoi desu. ちょっとおもいです。

> It's a bit heavy.

Ms. Smith wants a bit cheaper one, so she says

Mō sukoshi yasui no wa arimasu ka.
もうすこしやすいのはありますか。

> Do you have a bit cheaper one?

"**Mō sukoshi** もうすこし" or "**mō chotto** もうちょっと" means "a bit more." "**No** の" after an adjective means "one."
So "**mō sukoshi yasui no** もうすこしやすいの" means "a bit cheaper one."

If you want a slightly bigger one, you ask;

Mō chotto (or **Mō sukoshi**) **ōkii no wa arimasu ka.**
もうちょっと（もうすこし）おおきいのはありますか。

Practice Dialogue 3

🎧 Track3-9

Let's practice Sumisu san's part!

Sumisu	(Say "Excuse me. How much is this?")
Omise no hito	15,000 (ichiman gosen) en desu.
Sumisu	(Say "I see. It is a bit expensive. (Do you have) slightly cheaper one?")
Omise no hito	Kochira wa ikaga desu ka. 10,000 (ichiman) en desu.
Sumisu	(Say, "That sounds good. But it is a bit small. Is there (Do you have) size 11?)
Omise no hito	Hai. Sukoshi omachi kudasai. Kochira desu.
Sumisu	(Ask "May I try it on?")
Omise no hito	Hai. Shichaku shitsu wa achira desu.
Sumisu	(Say thank you)

Super!

Let's give it a try to play an "omise no hito" part.

Sumisu	Sumimasen. Kore wa ikura desu ka.
Omise no hito	(Tell her the price is 15,000 yen)
Sumisu	Sō desu ka. Chotto takai desu. Mō sukoshi yasui no wa arimasuka.
Omise no hito	(Say "How about this? It is 10,000 yen.")
Sumisu	Ii desu ne. Demo chotto chiisai desu. Jūichigō wa arimasu ka.
Omise no hito	(Say "Yes. Wait for a moment. Here it is.")
Sumisu	Shichaku shite mo ii desu ka.
Omise no hito	(Say, "Yes. The fitting room is over there.")
Sumisu	Arigatō gozaimasu.

Well done!

Related Vocabulary   Deck3

Here I show you some words of the things that you might buy in Japan!

Things

🎧 Track3-10

book	**hon**	ほん　本
dictionary	**jisho**	じしょ 辞書
magazine	**zasshi**	ざっし 雑誌
newspaper	**shinbun**	しんぶん 新聞
pocket diary	**techō**	てちょう　　手帳
stationary	**bunbōgu**	ぶんぼうぐ　文房具
pencil	**enpitsu**	えんぴつ　　鉛筆
ballpoint pen	**bōrupen**	ボールペン
mechanical pencil	**shāpu penshiru**	シャープペンシル
eraser	**keshigomu**	けしゴム　　消しゴム
card	**kādo**	カード
notebook	**nōto**	ノート
watch / clock	**tokei**	とけい 時計
umbrella	**kasa**	かさ　傘
camera	**kamera**	カメラ
computer	**konpyūtā**	コンピューター
PC (personal computer)	**pasokon**	パソコン
tablet	**taburetto**	タブレット
television	**terebi**	テレビ

radio	**rajio**	ラジオ
mobile phone	**keitai denwa**	けいたいでんわ 携帯電話
smart phone	**sumāto fon**	スマートフォン
car	**kuruma**	くるま 車
table	**tēburu**	テーブル
chair	**isu**	いす
bed	**beddo**	ベッド
clothes	**yōfuku**	ようふく 洋服
coat	**kōto**	コート
jacket	**jaketto**	ジャケット
trousers	**zubon**	ズボン
jeans	**jiinzu**	ジーンズ
skirt	**sukāto**	スカート
T-shirt	**Tshatsu**	T シャツ
dress	**wanpiisu**	ワンピース
shirt	**shatsu**	シャツ
sweater	**sētā**	セーター
socks	**kutsushita**	くつした 靴下
underwear	**shitagi**	したぎ 下着
shoes	**kutsu**	くつ 靴
boots	**būtsu**	ブーツ
bag	**kaban**	かばん

Speaking practice

 Track3-11

Imagine you are shopping now and need some help from a shop clerk. Let's speak in Japanese.

1) I want to buy a shirt.
2) I want to buy a car.
3) I want to buy two erasers.
4) Where are magazines?
5) Where are tablets?
6) How much is it?

Well done!

Listening practice

 Track3-12

Listen to the conversations and find out what items are searched and where they are.

1) Item: the place:
2) Item: the place:
3) Item: the place:

Further practice

 Track3-13

Substitute the underlined words with the word(s) in parentheses.

1. A: Sumimasen. <u>Skāto</u> wa doko desu ka.

　すみません。スカートはどこですか。

　Excuse me. Where are skirts?

B: <u>Sangai</u> desu. さんがいです。They are on the third floor.

a) A (stationary) , B (6th floor)
b) A (coat), B (5th floor)
c) A (wine), B (basement, 1st floor)

2. A: Sumimasen. <u>Hon</u> wa doko desu ka.

すみません。ほんはどこですか。

Excuse me. Where is the book?

B: Tēburu no <u>ue</u> desu. テーブルのうえです。

It's on the table.

a) A (umbrella), B (under the bed)
b) A (dictionary), B (in front of TV)
c) A (newspaper), B (behind the PC)
d) A (watch), B (the right side of the mobile phone)
e) A (TV), B (the left side of the bed)

3. A: <u>Kore</u> wa ikura desu ka. これはいくらですか。

How much is it?

B: <u>150 (hyaku gojū) en</u> desu.　１５０えんです。

It's 150 yen.

a) A (that (near the listener)), B (200yen)
b) A (that (far from both the listener and the speaker),
   B (1,000yen)
c) A (this), B(10,000yen)
d) A (that (near the listener)), B (1,400yen)
e) A (that (far from both the listener and the speaker),
   B(23,000yen)

4. Chotto <u>takai</u> desu. Mō sukoshi <u>yasui</u> no wa arimasu ka.

ちょっとたかいです。もうすこしやすいのはありますか。

It's a bit expensive. Do you have a bit cheaper one?

a) (big/small)
b) (old/new)
c) (heavy/light)
d) (expensive/inexpensive)

5. Translate into Japanese

a) A: Excuse me. Where are the magazines?
   B: Magazines are over there. A: I see. Thank you.
b) The book is under the dictionary.
c) The mobile phone is next to the PC.
d) A: Excuse me. How much is this?
   B: 2,800 yen.
   A: I see. It is a bit expensive. Is there a slightly cheaper
      one?
   B: How about this? It is 1,500 yen.
   A: That's nice.
e) A: Where is the fitting room?
   B: There (near the listener)
   A: Thank you.
f) A: Three ice creams, please.
   B: 820 yen.

Katakana Reading Quiz 1 (Optional)

 Track3-14

Now it's time to learn reading Katakana! Again, it is totally optional, but it must be fun if you find how to pronounce your familiar words in Japanese!

Please write these Katakana words in rōmaji (English letters). Then listen to the recordings to check the answers. You can find the letter table in Chapter 0.

1) フランス　2) アメリカ　3) イタリア　4) ロシア
5) ケニア　　6) トルコ　　7) メキシコ　8) スペイン

9) インド   10) ワイン   11) コアラ   12) パンダ

13) ライオン 14) テレビ   15) カメラ   16) ナイフ

17) シャツ   18) ズボン   19) ペン   20) ピザ

21) パン

Key Sentences

🎧 Track3-15

Gyūnyū wa doko desu ka. ぎゅうにゅうはどこですか。

Where is milk?

Gyūnyū wa sakana uriba no tonari desu.

ぎゅうにゅうはさかなうりばのとなりです。

Milk is next to the fish section.

Sukāto wo kaitain desu ga. スカートをかいたいんですが。

I would like to buy a skirt.

Chotto takai desu. ちょっとたかいです。

It's a bit expensive.

Mō sukoshi yasui no wa arimasuka.

もうすこしやすいのはありますか。

Do you have a bit cheaper one?

Cultural Information - Shopping

You will find shopping in Japan fun and enjoyable, not only because of exotic items but also of good customer service. When you enter any Japanese shop, you will hear "**Irasshaimase** いらっしゃいませ (welcome)." When you leave, shop clerks will thank you for saying, "**Arigatō**

gozaimashita ありがとうございました (Thank you)" and sometimes escort you out of the store, even if you don't buy anything. Japanese shop clerks are helpful, enthusiastic, and well-trained, so please don't worry about communicating with them.

- Many Japanese still love to pay by cash, and you may find you cannot use a credit card at small stores and restaurants.

- In a supermarket, you put a small shopping basket in a trolley and put items in it. When you pay for them, you set the basket on a checkout counter, and then a cashier will scan the barcode on each item and put it in a different color basket. It indicates the items have been bought. Once you pay the bill, you will bring the basket to the table behind the counter and pack things in bags.

- Most supermarkets and department stores provide gift-wrapping services. If you buy some items as souvenirs and need to be gift-wrapped, ask a shop clerk,

Purezento nano de, tsutsunde morae masu ka.

プレゼントなので、つつんでもらえますか。

Could you wrap it as a present?

***puresento**, present

Chapter 4. Going out

Exploring a new place is a kind of adventure. You will find something interesting at every corner in Japan. However, it might sometimes be daunting to buy a ticket and get on a train in an unfamiliar place. You might be confused about which way to go. Most Japanese are happy to help you, especially if you ask them in Japanese! Please don't panic.

In this chapter, you will learn how to

- Describe how to go somewhere
- Ask which way you should go
- Understand and use time expressions

Do you have a camera and a travel guide in your pocket? Great! Let's go and explore Japan!

Nikkō Shinkyō

Dialogue 1: How do I get there? Dōyatte ikimasu ka?

🎧 Track4-1

Ms. Smith would like to go to Nikko on Sunday, but she doesn't know exactly how to get there. She asks Yamada san.

Sumisu	Sumimasen, Yamada san.　Nichiyōbi ni Nikkō e ikitain desu ga.
Yamada	Ii desu ne.
Sumisu	Dōyatte ikimasu ka.
Yamada	Chikatetsu de Asakusa eki e ikimasu. Soko de Tōbu sen no densha ni norikaemasu. Tōbu Nikkō eki de orimasu.
Sumisu	Chikatetsu no eki wa doko desu ka.
Yamada	Hoteru kara massugu itte kudasai. Eki wa kuroi biru no tonari ni arimasu.
Sumisu	Arigatō gozaimasu.

スミス	すみません、山田さん。日曜日に日光へ 行きたいんですが。
山田	いいですね。
スミス	どうやって 行きますか。
山田	地下鉄で 浅草駅へ 行きます。そこで東武線の 電車に 乗りかえます。東武日光駅で 降ります。
スミス	地下鉄の 駅はどこですか。
山田	ホテルからまっすぐ 行ってください。駅は 黒いビルのとなりにあります。

スミス	ありがとうございます。
Smith	Excuse me, Mr. Yamada. I would like to go to Nikko on Sunday.
Yamada	Sounds good.
Smith	How do I get there?
Yamada	You go to Asakusa station by subway. You change to the Tobu line there. You get off at Tobu Nikko eki.
Smith	Where is the subway station?
Yamada	From the hotel, go straight (please). The station is next to the black building.
Smith	Thank you very much.

Vocabulary Deck4

Nichiyōbi Sunday **ni** (particle indicating time) **- e**
ikitain desu ga I would like to go to – **dōyatte** how
ikimasu go **chikatetsu** subway **de** by means of
(particle indicating means) **eki** station **sokode** at that
place **Tōbu sen** Tōbu line **densha** train **–ni**
norikaemasu change (a train) **orimasu** get off **hoteru**
hotel **kara** from **massugu** straight **itte kudasai** please
go **kuroi** black **biru** building

Grammar and Expressions

🎧 Track4-2

1. Go to some place

"Go" is "**ikimasu** いきます" in Japanese. If you will go to
Nikkō, you say:

Nikkō e ikimasu. にっこうへいきます。

I will go to Nikkō.

(Place) e ikimasu. (Place) へいきます。

> I will go to (Place).

"**E へ**" is a particle that indicates a direction. Usually, the sound of "**e**" is written as"え" in Hiragana, but, for this particle, "へ" is used.

If you go to Nikkō <u>by train</u>, then you say:

<u>Densha de</u> Nikkō e ikimasu.

でんしゃでにっこうへいきます。

> I go to Nikkō by train.

(Transportation) de (place) e ikimasu.

(Transportation) で (place) へいきます。
> I will go to (place) by (transportation).

"**De で**" is a particle that indicates a means.

If you go to Nikkō <u>on Sunday</u>, you say:

<u>Nichiyōbi ni</u> Nikkō e ikimasu.

にちようびににっこうへいきます。

(Time expression) ni (place) e ikimasu.

(Time expression) に (place) へいきます
> I will go to (place) on (time expression).

"**Ni に**" is a particle that indicates time.
Can you see each particle conveys different information?

If you want to say, "I would like to go to Nikkō," and would like to get some help from the listener, use "**ikitain desu ga**

いきたいんですが."

Nikkō e ikitain desu ga. にっこうへいきたいんですが。

I want to go to Nikko.

Then you ask, "how do I get there?"

Dōyatte ikimasu ka. どうやっていきますか。

How do I get there?

And you might get the answer, for example:

Takushii de ikimasu.　タクシーでいきます。

You go by taxi.

2. Transportation

To go somewhere, you need transportation.
Here is a list of some types of transport.

train	**densha**	でんしゃ	電車
subway	**chikatetsu**	ちかてつ	地下鉄
Shinkansen (bullet train)			
	Shinkansen	しんかんせん	新幹線
car	**kuruma**	くるま	車
taxi	**takushii**	タクシー	
bus	**basu**	バス	
airplane	**hikōki**	ひこうき	飛行機
ship	**fune**	ふね	船

And some useful verbs,

get on (a train)　　　**(densha ni) norimasu**

（でんしゃに）のります

get off (a train)   **(densha wo) orimasu**

（でんしゃを）おります

change (from a subway to a train)

(chikatetsu kara densha ni) norikaemasu

（ちかてつからでんしゃに）のりかえます

"**Ni** に" is a particle that has several meanings. In this case, it indicates the arrival place of the movement.

"**Kara** から" is a particle that is similar to "from" in English.

Let me show you some example sentences.

Minato eki de densha ni norimasu.

みなとえきででんしゃにのります。

I get on a train at Minato station.

Umino eki de chikatetsu ni norikaemasu.

うみのえきでちかてつにのりかえます。

I change to the subway at Umino station.

Yamano eki de densha wo orimasu.

やまのえきででんしゃをおります。

I get off the train at Yamano station.

3. Direction

In this dialogue, Yamada san explains how to go to an underground station.

Let's check the vocabulary first.

junction	**kōsaten**	こうさてん	交差点
traffic lights	**shingō**	しんごう	信号

corner	**kado**	かど　角
straight	**massugu**	まっすぐ　真っ直ぐ

The position words in Chapter 3, such as "**migi** みぎ right" or "**hidari** ひだり left" are also useful.

If you would like to say, "Go straight from the hotel,"

Hoteru kara massugu <u>itte kudasai</u>.

ホテルからまっすぐ<u>いってください</u>。

From the hotel, <u>(Please) go</u> straight.

"**Kudasai** ください" means "please." When we describe the direction, we usually add "please" to show our politeness. "**Massugu itte kudasai** まっすぐいってください" means "please go straight."

Maybe you need to use "turn";

Singo wo migi ni <u>magatte kudasai</u>.

しんごうをみぎに<u>まがってください</u>。

<u>(Please) turn</u> right at the traffic lights.

Kado wo hidari ni <u>magatte kudasai</u>.

かどをひだりに<u>まがってください</u>。

<u>(Please) turn</u> left at the corner.

If you would like to describe where a place is, you can use the sentence structure we learned in Chapter3.

(Something) wa (noun) no (position) ni arimasu.

(Something) is (position) (noun).

So, if the station is next to the black building, you say,

Eki wa kuroi biru <u>no tonari ni</u> arimasu.

えきはくろいビルのとなりにあります。

If the station is inside the black building, you say:

Eki wa kuroi biru <u>no naka ni</u> arimasu.

えきはくろいビルのなかにあります。

Practice Dialogue 1

🎧 Track4-3

Imagine you would like to ask your Japanese colleague how to get to Nikkō. Let's begin!

Sumisu	(Say, "Excuse me, Mr. Yamada. I would like to go to Nikko on Sunday.")
Yamada	Ii desu ne.
Sumisu	(Ask, "How do I get there?")
Yamada	Chikatetsu de Asakusa eki ni ikimasu. Soko de Tōbu sen no densha ni norikaemasu. Tōbu Nikkō eki de orimasu.
Sumisu	(Ask where the underground station is.)
Yamada	Hoteru kara massugu itte kudasai. Eki wa kuroi biru no tonari ni arimasu.
Sumisu	(Thank him.)

Well done! Now, it's your turn to give Ms. Smith trip information.

Sumisu	Sumimasen, Yamada san. Nichiyōbi ni Nikkō ni ikitain desu ga.
Yamada	(Say, "Sounds good.")

Sumisu	Dōyatte ikimasu ka.
Yamada	(Say, "You go to Asakusa station by underground. You change to the Tobu line there. You get off at Tobu Nikko eki.")
Sumisu	Chikatetsu no eki wa doko desu ka.
Yamada	(Say, "Please go straight from the hotel. The station is next to a black building.")
Sumisu	Arigatō gozaimasu.

Great! Now you can explain how to go!

Dialogue 2: I would like to go to Asakusa station. Asakusa eki e ikitain desu ga.

🎧 Track4-4

Ms. Smith is now in a station.

Eki de

Sumisu	Sumimasen. Asakusa eki e ikitain desu ga, ikura desu ka.
Ekiin	180 (Hyaku hachijū) en desu. Kippu no jidōhanbaiki wa asoko desu.
Sumisu	Arigatō gozaimasu.

Eki no naka de

Sumisu	Sumimasen. Asakusa eki e ikitain desu ga, hōmu wa doko desu ka.
Onna no hito	Asakusa hōmen wa 2 (ni) bansen no hōmu desu.
Sumisu	Arigatō gozaimasu.

駅<ruby>で</ruby>

スミス	すみません。浅草駅へ 行きたいんですが、いくらですか。
駅員	１８０ 円です。きっぷの 自動販売機は あそこです。
スミス	ありがとうございます。

駅の 中で

スミス	すみません。浅草駅へ 行きたいんですが、ホームはどこですか。
女 のひと	浅草方面は 2番線のホームです。

スミス　　　　　　ありがとうございます。

At a station

Smith	Excuse me. I would like to go to Asakusa station. How much is it?
Station staff	It's 180 yen. The ticket machine is over there.
Smith	Thank you.

In a station

Smith	Excuse me. I would like to go to Asakusa station. Where is the platform?
Woman	The platform for the Asakusa-bound train is no.2.
Smith	Thank you.

Vocabulary Deck4

eki station　**kippu** ticket　**jidōhanbaiki** vending machine
hōmu platform　**hōmen** direction　**2 bansen** platform no.2

Grammar and Expressions

🎧 Track4-5

1. *ko/so/a/do*

We have learned "**kore** これ" in Chapter 2 and "**koko** ここ, **soko** そこ, **asoko** あそこ, **doko** どこ" at Chapter 3.

These words look similar, don't they? Here is a table.

	ko こ (near the speaker)	**so** そ (near the listener)	**a** あ (far)	**do** ど (question)
Thing	**kore** これ this	**sore** それ that	**are** あれ that	**dore** どれ which
Place	**koko** ここ here	**soko** そこ there	**asoko** あそこ over there	**doko** どこ where
Direction/ Place(polite)	**kochira** こちら this direction, here	**sochira** そちら that direction, there	**achira** あちら that direction, over there	**dochira** どちら which direction, where
Thing(+Noun)	**kono** N この N this N	**sono** N その N that N	**ano** N あの N that N	**dono** N どの N which N

You can use these words like this.

<u>Sore</u> wa ikura desu ka. それはいくらですか。

How much is <u>that</u>?

Hōmu wa <u>doko</u> desu ka. ホームはどこですか。

<u>Where</u> is a platform?

Shichaku shitsu wa <u>achira</u> desu.

しちゃくしつは<u>あちら</u>です。 The fitting room is <u>over there</u>.

<u>Kono</u> michi wo massugu itte kudasai.

このみちをまっすぐいってください。

Please go straight along <u>this</u> road.

Practice Dialogue 2

 Track4-6

It's time to speak to staff at a Japanese station and a stranger. You don't have to worry. They will be friendly and kind. Let's begin!

Eki de

Sumisu	(Say. "Excuse me. I would like to go to Asakusa station. How much is it?")
Ekiin	180 (Hyaku hachijū) en desu. Kippu no jidōhanbaiki wa asoko desu.
Sumisu	(Thank him)

Eki no naka de

Sumisu	(Ask, "Excuse me. I would like to go to Asakusa station. Where is the platform?")
Onna no hito	Asakusa hōmen wa 2 (ni) bansen no hōmu desu.
Sumisu	(Thank her.)

Wonderful!
Now let's try Ekiin and Onna no hito.

Eki de

Sumisu	Sumimasen. Asakusa eki e ikitain desu ga, ikura desu ka.
Ekiin	(Say, "It's 180 yen. The ticket machine is over there.")
Sumisu	Arigatō gozaimasu.

Eki no naka de

Sumisu	Sumimasen. Asakusa eki e ikitain desu ga, hōmu wa doko desu ka.
Onna no hito	(Say, "The platform for the Asakusa-bound train is no.2.")
Sumisu	Arigatō gozaimasu.

Superb!

Dialogue 3: Where is the toilet? Toire wa doko desu ka.

 Track4-7

Ms. Smith is now in Nikko. She would like to go to Tōshōgū, a famous shrine in Nikko. She looks at her map but is not sure which way to go.

Nikkō de

Sumisu	Sumimasen. Tōshōgū wa doko desu ka.
Otoko no hito	Kono michi wo massugu itte kudasai.
Sumisu	Arigatō gozaimasu.

Tōshōgū no mae de

Sumisu	Sumimasen. Shashin wo onegaishimasu.
Onna no hito	Ii desu yo.
Sumisu	Arigatō gozaimasu.

Shashin no ato de

Sumisu	Ano, sumimasen.
Onna no hito	Hai, nan desu ka.
Sumisu	Toire wa doko desu ka.
Onna no hito	Ano kado wo migi ni magatte kudasai.
Sumisu	Arigatō gozaimasu.

日光で

スミス	すみません。東照宮はどこですか。
おとこのひと	この道をまっすぐ行ってください。
スミス	ありがとうございます。

東照宮の前で

スミス	すみません。写真をお願いします。
女のひと	いいですよ。

スミス　　　　　　　ありがとうございます。

写真の後で

スミス　　　　　　　あの、すみません。

女のひと　　　　　　はい、なんですか。

スミス　　　　　　　トイレはどこですか。

女のひと　　　　　　あの角を右に曲がってください。

スミス　　　　　　　ありがとうございます。

At Nikkō
Smith   Excuse me. Where is Tōshōgū?
Man   (Please) go straight along this road.
Smith   Thank you.

In front of Tōshōgū
Smith   Excuse me. Please could you take a
                 photograph (of me).
Woman   OK.
Smith   Thank you.

After taking some photos
Smith   Um, excuse me.
Woman   Yes?
Smith   Where is the toilet?
Woman   (Please) turn right at that corner.
Smith   Thank you.

Vocabulary ⬜ Deck4

Tōshōgū The biggest shrine in Nikkō **kono** this   **michi**
road, street   **shashin** photograph   **ii desu yo** OK. I'll do
it for you.   **ato** after   **ano** um   **toire** toilet
kado corner   **magatte kudasai** please turn cf **magarimasu**
turn

Grammar and Expressions

🎧 Track4-8

1. Please could you take a photograph (of me)

When Ms. Smith would like to ask a lady to take a photo, she says:

Shashin wo onegaishimasu. しゃしんをおねがいします。

(lit.)Photo, please.

"**Wo onegaishimasu.**" is a very useful expression. We have used this expression already.

When Yamada san asked the bill in Chapter 2, he said:

Okaikei wo onegaishimasu.

おかいけいをおねがいします。The bill, please.

When Ms. Smith ordered two hamburgers, she said:

Hanbāgā wo futatsu onegaishimasu.

ハンバーガーをふたつおねがいします。

Two hamburgers, please.

To order or to ask something, simply say "**(something) wo onegaishimasu** (something)をおねがいします"!

Practice Dialogue 3

 Track4-9

Imagine you are walking in Nikko alone, and you need some help. You decide to ask a stranger to help in Japanese. It will be great Japanese practice for you! Let's practice Sumisu san's part.

Sumisu	(Say, "Excuse me. Where is Tōshōgū?")
Otoko no hito	Kono michi wo massugu itte kudasai.
Sumisu	(Thank him)
Sumisu	(Say, "Excuse me. Photograph, please.")
Onna no hito	Ii desu yo.
Sumisu	(Thank her)
Sumisu	(Say, "Um, excuse me.")
Onna no hito	Hai, nan desu ka.
Sumisu	(Ask her, "Where is the toilet?")
Onna no hito	Ano kado wo migi ni magatte kudasai.
Sumisu	(Thank her)

Great! You should be proud of yourself!
Now, let's practice Otoko no hito and Onna no hito. You might have a chance to help others in Japan! You never know!

Sumisu	Sumimasen. Tōshōgū wa doko desu ka.
Otoko no hito	(Say, "Please go straight along this road.")
Sumisu	Arigatō gozaimasu.
Sumisu	Sumimasen. Shashin wo onegaishimasu.
Onna no hito	(Say, "OK.")
Sumisu	Arigatō gozaimasu.
Sumisu	Ano, sumimasen.
Onna no hito	(Say, "Yes?")

Sumisu	Toire wa doko desu ka.
Onna no hito	(Say, "Please turn right at that corner.")
Sumisu	Arigatō gozaimasu.

Good Job!

Related Vocabulary Deck4

Place

🎧 Track4-10

When you need to ask where a supermarket or a post office is, please use these words.

bank	**ginkō**	ぎんこう　銀行
post office	**yūbinkyoku**	ゆうびんきょく　郵便局
museum	**hakubutsukan**	はくぶつかん　博物館
art gallery	**bijutsukan**	びじゅつかん　美術館
library	**toshokan**	としょかん　図書館
cinema	**eigakan**	えいがかん　映画館
zoo	**dōbutsuen**	どうぶつえん　動物園
Buddhist temple	**otera**	おてら　お寺
Shinto shrine	**jinja**	じんじゃ　神社
Christian church	**kyōkai**	きょうかい　教会
swimming pool	**pūru**	プール
park	**kōen**	こうえん　公園
embassy	**taishikan**	たいしかん　大使館
police box	**kōban**	こうばん　交番
fire station	**shōbōsho**	しょうぼうしょ　消防署
parking lot	**chūshajō**	ちゅうしゃじょう　駐車場

university	**daigaku**	だいがく　大学
school	**gakkō**	がっこう　学校
butcher	**nikuya**	にくや　肉屋
fishmonger	**sakanaya**	さかなや　魚屋
bakery	**panya**	パンや　パン屋
liquor shop	**sakaya**	さかや　酒屋
vegetable shop	**yaoya**	やおや　八百屋
book shop	**honya**	ほんや　本屋
pharmacy	**kusuriya**	くすりや　薬屋
supermarket	**sūpā**	スーパー
department store	**depāto**	デパート
café	**kafe**	カフェ
	kissaten	きっさてん　喫茶店
restaurant	**resutoran**	レストラン
convenience store	**konbini**	コンビニ
hospital	**byōin**	びょういん　病院
bus stop	**basutei**	バスてい　バス停
taxi stand	**takushii noriba**	タクシーのりば
		タクシー乗り場

Time expressions 1

 Track4-11

I show you a massive list of time expressions. I don't want you to be discouraged, though. Let's learn them together gradually. And please remember. You can download ready-made e-flash cards to memorize them quickly!

Days of the week

First, let's check the days of the week.

Sunday	**nichiyōbi**	にちようび	日曜日
Monday	**getsuyōbi**	げつようび	月曜日
Tuesday	**kayōbi**	かようび	火曜日
Wednesday	**suiyōbi**	すいようび	水曜日
Thursday	**mokuyōbi**	もくようび	木曜日
Friday	**kinyōbi**	きんようび	金曜日
Saturday	**doyōbi**	どようび	土曜日
What day of the week	**nanyōbi**	なんようび	何曜日

So, if you would like to ask, "what day is today?"

Kyō wa <u>nanyōbi</u> desu ka.　きょうはなんようびですか。

What day is today?

And if today is Wednesday, the answer is,

<u>**Suiyōbi**</u> **desu.**　すいようびです。It's Wednesday.

See, it's easy!

Years

🎧 Track4-12

You have already learned numbers, so years are good practice. In Japanese, we read "1982" as "1,982", while in English, you read "1982" as "19" and "82".

1982　**sen kyūhyaku hachijū ni nen**
せんきゅうひゃくはちじゅうにねん　　1982 年

| 2020 | **nisen nijū nen** | にせんにじゅうねん | 2020年 |
| what year | **nan nen** | なんねん | 何年 |

<u>Nisen nijū nen</u> ni Tokyō orinpikku ga arimasu.

<u>にせんにじゅうねん</u>に とうきょうオリンピックがあります。

Tokyo Olympics will take place in 2020.

Months

🎧 Track4-13

In English, each month has a name like "January." In Japanese, we just count them. For example, January is the first month of a year, so we call it as "**ichigatsu** いちがつ (first month)." It's easy, isn't it?

January	**ichigatsu**	いちがつ	一月
February	**nigatsu**	にがつ	二月
March	**sangatsu**	さんがつ	三月
April	**shigatsu**	しがつ	四月
May	**gogatsu**	ごがつ	五月
June	**rokugatsu**	ろくがつ	六月
July	**shichigatsu**	しちがつ	七月
August	**hachigatsu**	はちがつ	八月
September	**kugatsu**	くがつ	九月
October	**jūgatsu**	じゅうがつ	十月
November	**jūichigatsu**	じゅういちがつ	十一月
December	**jūnigatsu**	じゅうにがつ	十二月
which month	**nangatsu**	なんがつ	何月

Hachigatsu ni Nihon e ikimasu.

はちがつににほんへいきます。

In August, I will go to Japan.

Days of the month

🎧 Track4-14

In general, days of the month are just a number + "**nichi** に
ち." For example, 17th is "**jūshichi** じゅうしち" +"**nichi** に
ち." There are some tricky bits, though. From 1st to 10th and
for 14th, 20th, and 24th, we use special words. But they are
similar to the general counters we have already learned. For
example, the 3rd day is "**mikka** みっか" and the general
counter for three is "**mittsu** みっつ."

1st	**tsuitachi**	ついたち	一日
2nd	**futsuka**	ふつか	二日
3rd	**mikka**	みっか	三日
4th	**yokka**	よっか	四日
5th	**itsuka**	いつか	五日
6th	**muika**	むいか	六日
7th	**nanoka**	なのか	七日
8th	**yōka**	ようか	八日
9th	**kokonoka**	ここのか	九日
10th	**tōka**	とおか	十日
11th	**jūichinichi**	じゅういちにち	十一日
12th	**jūninichi**	じゅうににち	十二日
13th	**jūsannichi**	じゅうさんにち	十三日
14th	**jūyokka**	じゅうよっか	十四日

15th	**jūgonichi**	じゅうごにち	十五日
16th	**jūrokunichi**	じゅうろくにち	十六日
17th	**jūshichinichi**	じゅうしちにち	十七日
18th	**jūhachinichi**	じゅうはちにち	十八日
19th	**jūkunichi**	じゅうくにち	十九日
20th	<u>**hatsuka**</u>	<u>はつか</u>	二十日
21st	**nijūichinichi**	にじゅういちにち	二十一日
22nd	**nijūninichi**	にじゅうににち	二十二日
23rd	**nijūsannichi**	にじゅうさんにち	二十三日
24th	<u>**nijūyokka**</u>	<u>にじゅうよっか</u>	二十四日
25th	**nijūgonichi**	にじゅうごにち	二十五日
26th	**nijūrokunichi**	にじゅうろくにち	二十六日
27th	**nijūshichinichi**	にじゅうしちにち	二十七日
28th	**nijūhachinichi**	にじゅうはちにち	二十八日
29th	**nijūkunichi**	にじゅうくにち	二十九日
30th	**sanjūnichi**	さんじゅうにち	三十日
31st	**sanjūichinichi**	さんじゅういちにち	三十一日
Which day of the month	**nannichi**	なんにち	何日

Tanjōbi wa itsu desu ka.   たんじょうびはいつですか。
   When is your birthday?   *__tanjōbi__ birthday   **itsu** when

Sangatsu kokonoka desu.   さんがつここのかです。
                              It's 9th of March.

Today, Tomorrow, etc

🎧 Track4-15

Finally, I'll introduce time expressions relative to the current time like "last week," "next month," or so on.

	last	this	next
day	**kinō**	**kyō**	**ashita**
	きのう	きょう	あした
	昨日	今日	明日
	yesterday	today	tomorrow
week	**senshū**	**konshū**	**raishū**
	せんしゅう	こんしゅう	らいしゅう
	先週	今週	来週
	last week	this week	next week
month	**sengetsu**	**kongetsu**	**raigetsu**
	せんげつ	こんげつ	らいげつ
	先月	今月	来月
	last month	this month	next month
year	**kyonen**	**kotoshi**	**rainen**
	きょねん	ことし	らいねん
	去年	今年	来年
	last year	this year	next year

Bear in mind that the particle "**ni** に" is not used with these words.

Itsu Rondon e ikimasu ka.   いつロンドンへいきますか。

　　　　　　　　　　　　　　　When will you go to London?

<u>**Raigetsu** ikimasu.</u> <u>らいげつ</u>いきます。 I'll go next month.

Phew! We have learned A LOT!   Well done!

Speaking practice

🎧 Track4-16

Can you say these conversations in Japanese?

1) A: Where is the post office?
   B: (Please) turn right at those traffic lights over there.
   A: Thank you.

2) A: I would like to go to the art gallery. How do I get there?
   B: (Please) go straight along this road. The art gallery is on
      the right-hand side of the bank.
   A: Thank you.

3) (at a train station)
   A: I would like to go to Nagoya station. Where is the
      platform?
   B: The platform for the Nagoya-bound train is no.5.
   A: Thank you.

Did you get it? Please listen to the answers and repeat them.

Listening practice

 Track4-17

1) Please listen to Ms. Smith asking Mr. Yamada about transportation and fill in the blanks based on the information you hear.

Sumisu san wa (   )ni (   )de
(   )e ikimasu.

2) Listen to Ms. Smith trying to find her way. Where does she want to go, and which platform should she go to?

The place she wants to go is (   )
The platform number is (   )

3) Listen to Ms. Smith buying a ticket. Where does she want to go and how much is the ticket?

The place she wants to go is (   )
The ticket price is (   )

Further practice

 Track4-18
Substitute the underlined words with the alternatives given.

1. <u>Nichiyōbi</u> ni <u>Nikkō</u> e ikitain desu ga.
　　にちようびににっこうへいきたいんですが。
                    I would like to go to Nikko on Sunday.

a) (Tuesday/Yokohama)
b) (Friday/ Kyōto)
c) (Thursday/ Fukuoka)
d) (Saturday / Kanazawa)
e) (Monday/ Sapporo)
f) (Wednesday/ Sendai)

g) (Sunday/ Kagawa)

2. <u>Chikatetsu</u> de <u>Asakusa</u> e ikimasu.

ちかてつであさくさへいきます。

I will go to Asakusa by subway.

a) (Train/ Ginza)
b) (Taxi/ Shibuya)
c) (Bus/ Shinjuku)
d) (Car/ Nakano)
e) (Subway/ Ueno)

3. ex1) <u>Asakusa</u> de <u>chikatetsu</u> <u>ni norimasu</u>.

あさくさでちかてつにのります。

I will get on a subway at Asakusa.

ex2) <u>Nikkō</u> de <u>densha</u> <u>wo orimasu</u>.

にっこうででんしゃをおります。

I will get off a train at Nikko.

a) (Narita/ airplane/ get off)
b) (Chiba/ bus/ get on)
c) (Yoyogi/ taxi/ get off)
d) (Tokushima/ ship/ get on)
e) (Iwami/ train/ get off)

4. ex) <u>Kōsaten</u> wo <u>massugu itte</u> kudasai.

こうさてんをまっすぐいってください。

Please go straight through the junction.

a) (traffic signal/ turn right)
b) (that(far) corner/ turn left)
c) (this road/ go straight)
d) (that (far) traffic signal/ turn left)

5. ex) A: Sumimasen. <u>Asakusa</u> eki e ikitain desu ga, ikura desu ka.

すみません。あさくさえきへいきたいんですが、

いくらですか。

Excuse me. I would like to go to Asakusa station. How much is it?

B: <u>180 (hyaku hachijū) en</u> desu.　<ruby>ひゃくはちじゅう</ruby> 180 えんです。

It's 180 yen.

a) A: (Yonago) B: (15,000yen)
b) A: (Toyama) B: (2,600yen)
c) A: (Nara)   B: (580yen)

6. A: Tanjōbi wa itsu desu ka. たんじょうびはいつですか。

When is your birthday?

B: <u>Gogatsu itsuka</u> desu.　ごがついつかです。

It's May the 5th.

a) (4th June)
b) (7th September)
c) (6th December)
d) (8th March)
e) (Your birthday)

7. Translate into Japanese

a) A: When is your birthday?
    B: October 14th.
b) A: What day is today?
    B: Thursday.
c) A: Excuse me. I would like to go to Ginza, how much is it?
    B: 230 yen.
d) A: Where is the shintō shrine?
    B: Please go straight at that junction over there.
e) A: Where is the park?
    B: Next to the police box.
f) A: Excuse me. Please could you take a photograph?
    B: All right.

Katakana Reading Quiz 2 (Optional)

🎧 Track4-19

In this quiz, I include many long vowels. When we write long vowels in Katakana, we use "ー." Let's try.

1) バナナ   2) パイナップル   3) マンゴー 4) キャベツ
5) グレープフルーツ 6) コンピューター 7) ヘリコプター
8) イギリス 9) カナダ 10) ギター 11) ゲーム 12) オランダ
13) チョコレート   14) バレンタインデー 15) ビオラ
16) オーストリア 17) ケーキ 18) アイスクリーム
19) コーヒー 20) フルート 21) ポケット

Key Sentences

🎧 Track4-20

Nichiyōbi ni Nikkō e ikitain desu ga.

にちようびににっこうへいきたいんですが。

I would like to go to Nikkō on Sunday.

Chikatetsu de Asakusa eki e ikimasu.

ちかてつであさくさえきへいきます。

You will go to Asakusa station by subway.

Hoteru kara massugu itte kudasai.

ホテルからまっすぐいってください。

Please go straight from the hotel.

Eki wa kuroi biru no tonari ni arimasu.

えきはくろいビルのとなりにあります。

The station is next to the black building.

Toire wa doko desu ka.   トイレはどこですか。

Where is the toilet?

Ano kado wo migi ni magatte kudasai.

あのかどをみぎにまがってください。

> Please turn right at that corner.

Cultural Information – Visiting Buddhism temples and Shintō shrines

Once you come to Japan, you will visit some Buddhism temples and Shintō shrines. Many of them are popular tourist destinations, but also, they are places of worship. If you know how to show your respect for such sacred sites, it would be more exciting and enjoyable to visit.

How to visit a Shinto shrine

- Pass through the "**torii** とりい" gate.

- Clean your hands and mouth by a ladle provided at a water basin called "**chōzuya** ちょうずや."
  1. Take a ladle on your right hand, scoop up water, and sprinkle water over your left hand.
  2. Pass a ladle from your right hand to your left hand, ladle up the water, and sprinkle water over your right hand.
  3. Pass a ladle back to your right hand, scoop up water, pour some water in your left hand, and wash your mouth.
  4. Finally, tip the ladle to rinse it off.

- In front of the main building, you make a wish.
  1. Throw some money in an offering box called "**saisen bako** さいせんばこ."
  2. Pull the ribbon or rope and ring the bell three times.
  3. Bow 90 degrees twice

4. Clap your hands twice
5. Make a wish in your heart without speaking.
6. Bow once more.

How to visit a Buddhism temple

- Pass through a huge gate called "**sanmon** さんもん"

- If you find "**chōzuya** ちょうずや," follow the same procedure above.

- You may find a big incense burner. You can offer a bundle of incense sticks called "**osenkō** おせんこう." Once the smoke rises, fan the smoke toward yourself. The smoke is believed to have healing power and to bring good luck.

- At the main building, throw some money and ring the bell. Then put your hands together in front of your chest in a prayer position and make a wish silently.

chōzuya ちょうずや

Chapter 5. Asking for help

Sometimes an unexpected thing can happen, even in the most enjoyable moments. It is not fun, but we have to deal with it. One of the most common problems is something going wrong in your hotel. You may have to tell the hotel staff that there is something wrong with your room. Or you may be sick and need to get some medical advice. In any case, it will be easier for you to get help if you can ask in Japanese.

In this chapter, you will learn how to

- Explain a problem
- Describe your symptoms
- Seek medical help

Personally, I hope you don't experience any problems in Japan, but if you've been prepared, you can tackle these problems confidently. So let's practice, just in case.

Hotel staff at a reception

Dialogue 1: There is something wrong with the shower. Shawā no chōshi ga waruin desu ga.

🎧 Track5-1

Ms. Smith has trouble with the shower in her room.

Sumisu	Sumimasen. Shawā no chōshi ga waruin desu ga.
Hoteru no hito	Sō desu ka. Mōshiwake gozaimasen. Sugu ni naoshimasu.
Sumisu	Onegaishimasu.

スミス	すみません。シャワーの調子が悪いんですが。
ホテルのひと	そうですか。申し訳ございません。すぐに直します。
スミス	お願いします。

Smith	Excuse me. There is something wrong with the shower.
Hotel staff	I see. I am sorry. We will soon fix it.
Smith	Please.

Vocabulary 📑 Deck5

shawā shower   **chōshi** condition   **warui** bad
sō desu ka. I see. I understand. **mōshiwake gozaimasen.** I
am sorry (polite)   **sugu ni** immediately   **naoshimasu**
fix

Grammar and Expressions

 Track5-2

1. *shawā no chōshi ga waruin desu ga.*

In this dialogue, Ms. Smith says,

Shawā no chōshi ga waruin desu ga.

シャワーのちょうしがわるいんですが。

> There is something wrong with the shower.

As we learned in Chapter 3, "**-n desu ga** -んですが" means the speaker needs some help from the listener. In this dialogue, Ms. Smith would like the hotel staff to fix the problem.

If you would like just to mention something is wrong, you say:

(Something) no chōshi ga warui desu.

(Something) のちょうしがわるいです。

> (Lit.) The condition of (something) is bad.

Or if something is good, you can say:

(Something) no chōshi ga ii desu.

(Something)のちょうしがいいです。

> The condition of (something) is good.

"**Chōshi** ちょうし" literally means condition. You can use this expression for something functional like your body, your job, or your machines.

Karada no chōshi ga ii desu. からだの ちょうしがいいです。

> (Lit. The condition of my body is good.) I am healthy.
> *karada body

Pasokon no chōshi ga warui desu.

パソコンのちょうしがわるいです。

The PC has some problems.

Shigoto no chōshi wa dōdesu ka.

しごとのちょうしはどうですか。

How is your work?
*dōdesu ka. How is ...?

If your work is excellent, you say,

"**Totemo Ii desu.** とてもいいです。"

If so-so, "**Māmā desu.** まあまあです。"

If not so good, "**Amari yokunai desu.** あまりよくないです。"

Practice Dialogue 1

🎧 Track5-3

It would not be nice if the shower in your hotel room doesn't work well. Let's ask to have it fixed.

Sumisu	(Say, "Excuse me. There is something wrong with the shower.")
Hoteru no hito	Sō desu ka. Mōshiwake gozaimasen. Sugu ni naoshimasu.
Sumisu	(Say, "Please.")

Next, you play Hoteru no hito's part. Remember to be polite to your customer.

Sumisu	Sumimasen. Shawā no chōshi ga waruin desu ga.
Hoteru no hito	(Say, "I see. I am sorry. We will soon fix it.")
Sumisu	Onegaishimasu.

Wonderful!

Dialogue 2: I have a stomach ache. Onaka ga itain desu ga.

🎧 Track5-4

Ms. Smith feels sick. She would like to go to the hospital. She goes to the front desk to ask where the hospital is.

Sumisu	Sumimasen. Onaka ga itain desu ga.
Hoteru no hito	Daijōbu desu ka.
Sumisu	Byōin wa doko desu ka.
Hoteru no hito	Byōin wa eki no chikaku desu. Takushii wo yobimasu ka.
Sumisu	Hai, onegaishimasu.

スミス	すみません。お腹が痛いんですが。
ホテルのひと	だいじょうぶですか。
スミス	病院はどこですか。
ホテルのひと	病院は駅の近くです。タクシーを呼びますか。
スミス	はい、お願いします。

Smith	Excuse me. I have a stomach ache.
Hotel staff	Are you all right?
Smith	Where is the hospital?
Hotel staff	The hospital is near the station. Shall I call a taxi?
Smith	Yes, please.

Vocabulary 📇 Deck5

onaka tummy, stomach **itai** painful **daijōbu** all right
byōin hospital **yobimasu** call

Grammar and Expressions

 Track5-5

1. Illness

In this dialogue, Ms. Smith says,

Onaka ga itain desu ga. おなかがいたいんですが。

I have a stomach ache.

Again, **"-n desu ga** -んですが**"** means you need some help.

If you would like to describe any pain, use this expression.

(body part) ga itai desu. (body part)がいたいです。

I have pain in (body part)

For example:

Atama ga itai desu. あたまがいたいです。

I have a headache. *atama head

Nodo ga itai desu. のどがいたいです。

I have a sore throat. *nodo throat

If you need some help, you say,

Atama ga itain desu ga. あたまがいたいんですが。

I have a headache.

Nodo ga itain desu ga. のどがいたいんですが。

I have a sore throat.

Let's see other expressions related to illness.

Netsu ga arimasu.   ねつがあります。

I have a fever. *netsu fever

Hanamizu ga demasu. はなみずがでます。

I have a runny nose. *hanamizu (lit. nose water) a runny nose

Seki ga demasu.   せきがでます。

I have a cough. *seki cough

Hakike ga shimasu. はきけがします。

I feel nauseous. *hakike nauseous

Samuke ga shimasu. さむけがします。

I feel a chill. *samuke chill

Memai ga shimasu. めまいがします。

I feel dizzy. *memai dizzy

If you need some help, you say,

Netsu ga arun desu ga.   ねつがあるんですが。

I have a fever.

Hanamizu ga derun desu ga. はなみずがでるんですが。

I have a runny nose.

Seki ga derun desu ga.   せきがでるんですが。

I have a cough.

Hakike ga surun desu ga. はきけがするんですが。

I feel nauseous.

Samuke ga surun desu ga. さむけがするんですが。

I feel a chill.

Memai ga surun desu ga.   めまいがするんですが。

I feel dizzy.

Practice Dialogue 2

 Track5-6

Now please take Ms. Smith's role.

Sumisu	(Say, "Excuse me. I have a stomach ache.")
Hoteru no hito	Daijōbu desu ka.
Sumisu	(Ask, "Where is the hospital?")
Hoteru no hito	Byōin wa eki no chikaku desu. Takushii wo yobimasu ka.
Sumisu	(Say, "Yes, please.")

Well done! Next, let's play the "Hoteru no hito"'s role.

Sumisu	Sumimasen. Onaka ga itain desu ga.
Hoteru no hito	(Say, "Are you all right?")
Sumisu	Byōin wa doko desu ka.
Hoteru no hito	(Say," A hospital is near a station. Shall I call a taxi?")
Sumisu	Hai, onegaishimasu.

Superb!

Dialogue 3: I want some medicine. Kusuri ga hoshiin desu ga.

 Track5-7

Ms. Smith is not well, so she goes to a pharmacy.

Kusuriya de

Sumisu	Sumimasen. Kusuri ga hoshiin desu ga.
Kusuriya no hito	Netsu ga arimasu ka.
Sumisu	Sukoshi netsu ga arimasu. Nodo ga itai desu.
Kusuriya no hito	Hanamizu ga demasu ka.
Sumisu	Amari demasen.
Kusuriya no hito	Kono kusuri wa ikaga desu ka. Nodo no itami ni ii desu.
Sumisu	Arigatō gozaimasu.

<ruby>薬<rt>くすりや</rt></ruby>屋で

スミス	すみません。<ruby>薬<rt>くすり</rt></ruby>がほしいんですが。
<ruby>薬<rt>くすり</rt></ruby>やのひと	<ruby>熱<rt>ねつ</rt></ruby>がありますか。
スミス	<ruby>少<rt>すこ</rt></ruby>し<ruby>熱<rt>ねつ</rt></ruby>があります。のどが<ruby>痛<rt>いた</rt></ruby>いです。
薬やのひと	<ruby>鼻水<rt>はなみず</rt></ruby>がでますか。
スミス	あまりでません。
薬やのひと	この<ruby>薬<rt>くすり</rt></ruby>はいかがですか。のどの<ruby>痛<rt>いた</rt></ruby>みにいいです。
スミス	ありがとうございます。

At a pharmacy

Smith	Excuse me. I'd like some medicine.
Pharmacist	Do you have a fever?

Smith	A little bit. I have a sore throat.
Pharmacist	Do you have a runny nose?
Smith	Not so much.
Pharmacist	How about this medicine? It is good for sore throats.
Smith	Thank you.

Vocabulary 　Deck5

kusuri medicine　　**(something) ga hoshiin desuga** I want (something)　**netsu** fever　**nodo** throat　**hanamizu** runny nose　**amari** not so much　**ii** good

Grammar and Expressions

🎧 Track5-8

1. Good for ....

In this dialogue, a pharmacist says,

(Kono kusuri wa) nodo no itami ni ii desu.
（このくすりは）のどのいたみにいいです。
　　　　　　　　(This medicine) is good for a sore throat.

(something) ni ii desu.　　(something) にいいです。
　　　　　　　　　　It is good for (something).

This expression can be used when something works as a remedy. For example:

Kore wa kaze ni ii desu. これはかぜにいいです。
　　　　　　　This is good for a cold. *kaze cold (illness)

Kono hon wa Nihongo no benkyō ni ii desu.

このほんはにほんごのべんきょうにいいです。

This book is good for Japanese study.

*Nihongo Japanese language **benkyō** study

Kono sukāto wa pātii ni ii desu.

このスカートはパーティーにいいです。

This skirt is good for parties. *pātii party

Practice Dialogue 3

🎧 Track5-9

Let's pretend to be Ms. Smith and go to a pharmacy.

Sumisu	(Say, "Excuse me. I'd like some medicine.")
Kusuriya no hito	Netsu ga arimasu ka.
Sumisu	(Say, "A little bit. I have a sore throat.")
Kusuriya no hito	Hanamizu ga demasu ka.
Sumisu	(Say, "Not so much.")
Kusuriya no hito	Kono kusuri wa ikaga desu ka. Nodo no itami ni ii desu.
Sumisu	(Thank her.)

OK? Good! Now let's be a pharmacist.

Sumisu	Sumimasen. Kusuri ga hoshiin desu ga.
Kusuriya no hito	(Ask, "Do you have a fever?")
Sumisu	Sukoshi netsu ga arimasu. Nodo ga itai desu.
Kusuriya no hito	(Ask," Do you have a runny nose?")
Sumisu	Amari demasen.
Kusuriya no hito	(Say, "How about this medicine. It is good for sore throat.")
Sumisu	Arigatō gozaimasu.

Great!

Related Vocabulary Deck5

In Dialogue 2 and 3, we learned how to explain when you are not well. It's helpful if you get familiar with Japanese body part words. I also show you the Kanji's for these words because you might see them in Japan. You don't have to memorize them, though!

Body parts

🎧 Track5-10

body	**karada** からだ　体
head	**atama** あたま　頭
face	**kao** かお　顔
eye	**me** め　目
nose	**hana** はな　鼻
mouth	**kuchi** くち　口
tooth / teeth	**ha** は　歯
ear	**mimi** みみ　耳
hair	**kami** かみ　髪
neck	**kubi** くび　首
throat	**nodo** のど　喉
shoulder	**kata** かた　肩
arm	**ude** うで　腕
hand	**te** て　手
finger	**yubi** ゆび　指
nail	**tsume** つめ　爪
elbow	**hiji** ひじ　肘

back	**senaka** せなか　背中
lower back	**koshi** こし　腰
tummy	**onaka** おなか　お腹
leg, foot	**ashi** あし　足
knee	**hiza** ひざ　膝
bone	**hone** ほね　骨

Illness

🎧 Track5-11

During your stay, you may need to tell the hotel staff or the waiter that you have some allergy and cannot eat a particular food.

allergy	**arerugii**	アレルギー
wheat	**komugi**	こむぎ
egg	**tamago**	たまご
nut	**nattsu**	ナッツ
soya	**daizu**	だいず

(something) arerugii desu. (something) アレルギーです。

　　　　　　　　　　　　I have (something) allergy.

(something) ga taberaremasen.

(something)がたべられません。

　　　　　　　　　　　　I cannot eat (something).

(something) ga nomemasen.

(something)がのめません。

　　　　　　　　　　　　I cannot drink (something).

For example,

Komugi arerugii desu. こむぎアレルギーです。

> I have a wheat allergy.

Komugi ga taberare masen. こむぎがたべられません。

> I cannot eat wheat.

Here are some illnesses and symptoms you might need to tell:

diabetes	**tōnyōbyō**	とうにょうびょう
asthma	**zensoku**	ぜんそく
anemia	**hinketsu**	ひんけつ
heyfever	**kafunshō**	かふんしょう
cold	**kaze**	かぜ
period pains	**seiritsū**	せいりつう
hangover	**futsuka yoi**	ふつかよい
motion sickness	**norimono yoi**	のりものよい
diarrhea	**geri**	げり
constipation	**benpi**	べんぴ
vomiting	**ōto**	おうと
eczema	**shisshin**	しっしん

(Illness/symptom) desu. (illness/symptom)です。

> I have (illness/symptom).

Kaze desu. かぜです。   I have a cold.

Time expressions 2

 Track5-12

We learned some time expressions in Chapter 4. What we will learn here are hours and minutes.

O'clock

1.00	**ichiji**	いちじ
2.00	**niji**	にじ
3.00	**sanji**	さんじ
4.00	<u>**yoji**</u>	<u>よじ</u>
5.00	**goji**	ごじ
6.00	**rokuji**	ろくじ
7.00	<u>**sichiji**</u>	<u>しちじ</u>
8.00	**hachiji**	はちじ
9.00	<u>**kuji**</u>	<u>くじ</u>
10.00	**jūji**	じゅうじ
11.00	**jūichiji**	じゅういちじ
12.00	**jūniji**	じゅうにじ

O'clock is "number + **ji** じ." Please be aware that 4.00 is called "**yoji** よじ," 7.00 "**shichiji** しちじ" and 9.00 "**kuji** くじ." So, how do we say minutes? Let's find out.

Minutes

1	<u>**ippun**</u>	<u>いっぷん</u>
2	**nifun**	にふん
3	<u>**sanpun**</u>	<u>さんぷん</u>

4	**yonpun**	よんぷん
5	**gofun**	ごふん
6	**roppun**	ろっぷん
7	**nanafun**	ななふん
8	**happun**	はっぷん
9	**kyūfun**	きゅうふん
10	**juppun**	じゅっぷん
20	**nijuppun**	にじゅっぷん
30	**sanjuppun** / han	さんじゅっぷん・はん
40	**yonjuppun**	よんじゅっぷん
50	**gojuppun**	ごじゅっぷん

About minutes, the basic rule is "number + **fun** ふん." However, you might have noticed there are lots of irregular words! You can see "**fun** ふん" become "**pun** ぷん," 4 minutes is "**yonpun** よんぷん," 7 minutes is "**nanafun** ななふん" and 9 minute is "**kyūfun** きゅうふん." They are all underlined above.

If you would like to ask what time it is now, you say,

Ima nanji desu ka. いまなんじですか。

What time is it now? *****ima** now **nanji** what time

If it is 3:00, the answer is,

Sanji desu.   さんじです。   It is 3.00.

If it is 2:30,

Niji sanjuppun desu.　にじさんじゅっぷんです。
Or
Niji han desu.　にじはんです。 *"han" means "half."

Speaking practice

🎧 Track5-13

1) What would you say if

- You had a headache?
- Your shoulders weren't in good condition?
- You had a chill?

2) Imagine you have pain in your lower back. Let's explain this to the hotel staff.

You:	(Excuse me. I have a pain in my lower back.)
Hotel staff:	(Are you all right?)
You:	(I would like to go to a pharmacy.)
Hotel staff:	(Please go straight along this road. The pharmacy is next to the bakery.)
You:	(Thank you.)

Listening practice

🎧 Track5-14
Listen to the conversation carefully and find out what is wrong.

1)

2)

3)

4)

5)

6)

Further practice

🎧 Track5-15
Substitute the underlined part(s) with the alternatives given.

1. <u>Shawā</u> no chōshi ga waruin desu ga.
  シャワーのちょうしがわるいんですが。

  There is something wrong with a shower.
a) (car)
b) (body)
c) (eye)
d) (stomach)
e) (TV)
f) (mobile phone)
g) (PC)

2. <u>Nodo ga itai desu.</u> のどがいたいです。

  I have a sore throat.

a) (have a tummy ache)
b) (have a headache)
c) (have a runny nose)
d) (feel nauseous)
e) (feel dizzy)
f) (have a cough)
g) (have a pain in my arm)
h) (have a pain in my knee)
i) (feel a chill)

3. <u>San ji</u> desu. さんじです。 It is 3.00.

a) 1.00
b) 4.00
c) 12.00
d) 7.00
e) 9.00
f) 3.10
g) 5.20
h) 11.40
i) 6.30
j) 8.50
k) 10.05
l) 2.15
m) 4.04
n) 7.07
o) 9.09

4. <u>Ano shingō</u> wo <u>hidari ni magatte</u> kudasai.
あのしんごうをひだりにまがってください。

Please turn left at that traffic signal.

a) (that(far) junction/ turn right)
b) (this corner/ turn left)
c) (this road/ go straight)
d) (those (far) traffic lights/ go straight)

5. A: <u>Byōin</u> wa doko desu ka. びょういんはどこですか。

Where is the hospital?

B: <u>Eki no chikaku</u> desu. えきのちかくです。

It is near the station.

a) A:(museum)
   B:(next to the library)
b) A:(bakery)
   B:(in front of the zoo)
c) A:(swimming pool)

B:(8th floor)

6. Translate into Japanese

a) A: Excuse me. There is something wrong with the smartphone.
   B: I see. I will soon fix it.
   A: Please.
b) A: How is your work?
   B: It's great.
c) A: Excuse me. I have a sore throat.
   B: Are you all right?
   A: I want medicine.
   B: How about this medicine. It is good for sore throat.
   A: Thank you.
d) A: When will you go to Sapporo?
   B: I will go next week.
e) A: Where is a toilet?
   B: It is on the 2nd floor.

Final Hiragana and Katakana Reading Quiz (Optional)

 Track5-16

Here is the last reading quiz! Give them a try!

1) ちゅうごく   2) はじめまして   3) ブロッコリー
4) かぎ 5) ボールペン 6) はさみ   7) りんご   8) セーター
9) トマト   10) アスパラガス 11) パソコン   12) トラッ
ク 13) ねこ   14) じしょ   15) ゼリー 16) たいこ
17) パトカー 18) フォーク 19) こんにちは
20) ありがとうございます 21) さようなら

Key Sentences

🎧 Track5-17

Shawā no chōshi ga waruin desu ga.

シャワーのちょうしがわるいんですが。

There is something wrong with the shower.

Onaka ga itain desu ga. おなかがいたいんですが。

I have a stomach ache.

Sukoshi netsu ga arimasu. すこしねつがあります。

I have a slight fever.

Nodo no itami ni ii desu. のどのいたみにいいです。

It is good for sore throat.

Cultural Information - Prevention of disease

Japanese has a reputation of obsession with cleanliness. We take off our shoes at the entrance of houses, schools, or even some public places. We have a bath every day. We love to learn how to keep clean and to prevent disease. After all, Japan is in a monsoon climate, very humid and hot during summer. It is the ideal condition for germs to spread. So we have to deal with it.

I show you several examples you may encounter during your stay in Japan.

- Mask (**masuku** マスク): If you visit Japan, especially in Winter and Spring, you can find many people, almost all people wearing white masks. We believe masks prevent pollen from coming in and also germs from spreading when we sneeze.

- Washing hands and gargling (**tearai to ugai** てあらい とうがい): Once you come back your home, you have to wash your hands and gargle. We believe gargling is essential to get rid of germs.

- Special toilet slippers (**toire no surippa** トイレのス リッパ): In a Japanese house, we take off our shoes at the entrance and wear slippers. If you would like to use a toilet, you take off your slippers before entering the toilet and wear special toilet slippers inside the toilet. You must not wear toilet slippers outside of the toilet. We think that the floor of the toilet is not clean enough. To prevent germs from spreading through the soles of the toilet slippers, we should change slippers.

- Blowing your nose (**hana wo kamu** はなをかむ): Blowing your nose in public is not acceptable. On the other hand, sniffling is OK. If you need to blow your nose, it is better to go somewhere private or at least to turn your face, to blow unnoticeably and to say "**Sumimasen** すみません." It is the same when you sneeze. If you blow your nose or sneeze in public, people around you kindly ignore it as if nothing happened, instead of pointing out the incident by saying like "god bless you." If you blow your nose, you must use a tissue, not a handkerchief. Handkerchiefs are for wiping your hands after handwashing, so they must be kept clean.

Well done!
You have finished **ALL** the chapters.
Hurrah for YOU!

Thank you!

Arigatō gozaimasu

ありがとうございます

Thank you so much for reading this book and learning Japanese together!

Don't forget to download your FREE Gifts!

Please go to the link below to download your special Full Audio Files and Ready-Made Anki e-Flash Cards for FREE.

http://www.funjapaneselearning.com/travelersfreegifts

How to use Anki

Anki was developed by Damien Elmes. This program helps you learn new words by heart. Anki works on windows, Mac, Linux. There are also smartphone versions; you can download this program for free, except for the iPhone version.

Step1. Install Anki program.

- Go to **https://apps.ankiweb.net/** to download the latest Anki.
- Select the right download for your computer.
- Download, Run and Install.

Step2. Download Anki e-Flash Cards with Audio.

- Go to the link above and install the deck files.
- Select the downloaded file and unzip it (the way to unzip could be different depending on your OS. For Windows, right-click and select "Extract All")
- Double-click on the file you unzipped to open it in the Anki program. Or open your Anki program, click the "Import File" icon at the bottom of the page and select the file.
- The decks will show up in your Anki deck list.

Step3. Learn your Deck.

- Click the deck you want to learn.
- Click on "Study Now" to start.
- Then first cue card appears.
- Answer the cue by yourself and press "show answer."
- Rate your answer by clicking the button "easy," "good," or "again."
- Continue until the "congratulations" message appears.

As you click the button like "easy," "good," or "again," the card will appear again after an appropriate interval time, depending on which button you press. For example, if you press the "easy" button, the card will come up again a few days later. If you press the "again" button, the card will come up within a few minutes. So you can learn each card by spaced repetition effectively until your brain absorbs all the words, and you can recall them easily.

You can customize the length of intervals by clicking the "option" button, which appears at the bottom of the screen when you open a deck.

If you would like to know more, see Anki User Manual:

https://docs.ankiweb.net/#/

Please Keep in Touch!

It would be an excellent opportunity to hear from you. Do you have any questions or comments? Please feel free to send me an e-mail. Do you have some exciting experiences in Japan? I would be more than happy to hear from you. Please share your story!

My e-mail is:

asuka@funjapaneselearning.com

I hope you have a great time in Japan.

Have a nice flight! **Itterasshai!** いってらっしゃい！

Asuka

Answers

Chapter 1.

Speaking practice

1) Kochira wa Kyashii san desu. Kyashii san wa Amerika jin desu. Nūyōku kara kimashita. Kyōshi desu.

こちらはキャシーさんです。キャシーさんはアメリカじんです。ニューヨークからきました。きょうしです。

2) Kochira wa Erikku san desu. Erikku san wa Furansu jin desu. Pari kara kimashita. Kenkyūsha desu.

こちらはエリックさんです。エリックさんはフランスじんです。パリからきました。けんきゅうしゃです。

3) Kochira wa Wan san desu. Wan san wa Chūgoku jin desu. Pekin kara kimashita. Toshibo de hataraite imasu.

こちらはワンさんです。ワンさんはちゅうごくじんです。ペキンからきました。とうしぼではたらいています。

4) Your answer

Listening practice

1) Hajimemashite. Akemi desu. Yokohama kara kimashita. Kenchikuka desu. Yoroshiku onegaishimasu.

はじめまして。あけみです。よこはまからきました。けんちくかです。よろしくおねがいします。

2) Kochira wa Jack san desu. Igirisu jin desu. Bengoshi desu.

こちらはジャックさんです。イギリスじんです。べんごしです。

3) Hajimemashite. Tōmasu desu. Ōsutoraria jin desu. Shidonii kara kimashita. Keisatsukan desu. Yoroshiku onegaishimasu.

はじめまして。トーマスです。オーストラリアじんです。シドニーからきました。けいさつかんです。よろしくおねがい

します。

4) Kochira wa Ishikawa san desu. Ishikawa san wa Nihonjin desu.
Kyōto kara kimashita. Gakusei desu.

こちらはいしかわさんです。いしかわさんはにほんじんです。
きょうとからきました。がくせいです。

5) Hajimemashite. Kondō desu. Fukuoka kara kimashita. Shufu
desu. Yoroshiku onegaishimasu.

はじめまして。こんどうです。ふくおかからきました。しゅ
ふです。よろしくおねがいします。

	name	nationality	hometown	occupation
1)	Akemi		Yokohama	architect
2)	Jack	British		lawyer
3)	Thomas	Australian	Sydney	policeman
4)	Ms. Ishikawa	Japanese	Kyoto	student
5)	Ms. Kondō		Fukuoka	housewife

Further practice

1.
a) A: Sumimasen. Hosoki san desu ka.

すみません。ほそきさんですか。

B: Hai, sō desu. はい、そうです。

b) A: Sumimasen. Aikawa san desu ka.

すみません。あいかわさんですか。

B: Iie, chigaimasu. いいえ、ちがいます。

c) A: Sumimasen. Harada san desu ka.

すみません。はらださんですか。

B: Hai, sō desu. はい、そうです。

d) A: Sumimasen. Suzuki san desu ka.

すみません。すずきさんですか。

B: Iie, chigaimasu. いいえ、ちがいます。

e) A: Sumimasen. Saitō san desu ka.

すみません。さいとうさんですか。

B: Hai, sō desu. はい、そうです。

2.

a) Hajimemashite. Akimoto desu. Fujiyama daigaku no kennkyūsha desu. Yoroshiku onegaishimasu.

はじめまして。あきもとです。ふじやまだいがくのけんきゅ

うしゃです。よろしくおねがいします。

b) Hajimemashite. Kishida desu. Hoshi byōin no kangoshi desu. Yoroshiku onegaishimasu.

はじめまして。きしだです。ほしびょういんのかんごしです。

よろしくおねがいします。

c) Hajimemashite. Garante desu. Maikurohādo no enjinia desu. Yoroshiku onegaishimasu.

はじめまして。ガランテです。マイクロハードのエンジニア

です。よろしくおねがいします。

d) Hajimemashite. Tānya desu. Honba no shain desu. Yoroshiku onegaishimasu.

はじめまして。ターニャです。ホンバのしゃいんです。よろ

しくおねがいします。

3. Doko kara kimashita ka. どこからきましたか。

a) Berurin kara kimashita. ベルリンからきました。

b) Rosanzerusu kara kimashita. ロサンゼルスからきました。

c) Amusuterudamu kara kimashita.

アムステルダムからきました。

d) Okinawa kara kimashita. おきなわからきました。

e) Madoriido kara kimashita. マドリードからきました。

4.

a) A: Ōsutoraria jin desu ka. オーストラリアじんですか。

B: Iie, Nyūjiirando jin desu.

いいえ、ニュージーランドじんです。

b) A: Chūgoku jin desu ka. ちゅうごくじんですか。

B: Iie, Kankoku jin desu. いいえ、かんこくじんです。

c) A: Furansu jin desu ka. フランスじんですか。

B: Iie, Kanada jin desu. いいえ、カナダじんです。

d) A: Supein jin desu ka. スペインじんですか。

B: Iie, Itaria jin desu. いいえ、イタリアじんです。

e) A: Mekishiko jin desu ka. メキシコじんですか。

B: Iie, Burajiru jin desu. いいえ、ブラジルじんです。

5.

a) Sumimasen. Honda san desu ka.

すみません。ほんださんですか。

Iie, chigaimasu. いいえ、ちがいます。

b) Hajimemashite. Saitō desu. Yoroshiku onegaishimasu.

はじめまして。さいとうです。よろしくおねがいします。

c) Buraun san wa Igirisu jin desu ka.

ブラウンさんはイギリスじんですか。

Iie, Shingapōru jin desu. いいえ、シンガポールじんです。

d) Aoki san wa sensei desu ka. あおきさんはせんせいですか。

Iie, gakusei desu. いいえ、がくせいです。

e) Kawai san wa byōin de hataraite imasu.

かわいさんはびょういんではたらいています。

f) Nishimoto san wa watashi no tomodachi desu.

にしもとさんはわたしのともだちです。

g) Airurando kara kimashita ka.

アイルランドからきましたか。

Iie, Oranda kara kimashita.

いいえ、オランダからきました。

Hiragana Reading Quiz

1) aki(autumn)   2) fuyu (winter)   3) haru (spring)
4) natsu (summer)   5) kuruma (car)   6) nihon (Japan)
7) shima (island)   8) chikatetsu (subway)   9) inu (dog)
10) yuki (snow)   11) tokei (watch/clock) 12) hon (book)
13) kasa (umbrella)   14) tsukue (desk)   15) isu (chair)
16) hasami (scissors) 17) yama (mountain) 18) sakana (fish)
19) niku (meat)   20) yasai (vegetable)   21) hana (flower)

Chapter 2.

Speaking practice

1) Karēraisu wo onegaishimasu.
   カレーライスをおねがいします。
2) Biiru wo onegaishimasu.
   ビールをおねがいします。
3) Piza to kōhii wo onegaishimasu.
   ピザとコーヒーをおねがいします。
4) Aisu kuriimu wo futatsu onegaishimasu.
   アイスクリームをふたつおねがいします。
5) Kōcha wo mittu onegaishimasu.
   こうちゃをみっつおねがいします。
6) Hotto doggu wo itsutsu onegaishimasu.
   ホットドッグをいつつおねがいします。
7) Yakizakana wo muttsu to yakiniku wo yottsu onegaishimasu.
   やきざかなをむっつとやきにくをよっつおねがいします。

Listening practice

1.

a) A: Sushi wo onegaishimasu. すしをおねがいします。

   Answer: sushi すし sushi

b) A: Kore wa nan desu ka. これはなんですか。

　B: Udon desu. うどんです。

　A: Sō desu ka. Ja, kore wo onegaishimasu.
　そうですか。じゃ、これをおねがいします。

　Answer: udon うどん udon

c) A: Irasshaimase. Okimari desu ka.
　いらっしゃいませ。おきまりですか。

　B: Hotto doggu wo onegaishimasu.
　ホットドックをおねがいします。

　Answer: Hotto doggu ホットドッグ hotdog

d) A: Onomimono wa ikaga desu ka.
　おのみものはいかがですか。

　B: Kōhii wo futatsu onegaishimasu.
　コーヒーをふたつおねがいします。

　Answer: Kōhii wo futatsu コーヒーをふたつ　2 coffee

2.

a) A: Sen en desu. せんえんです。　　It's 1,000 yen.

b) Sanzen gohyaku en desu. さんぜんごひゃくえんです。
It's 3,500 yen.

c) Gosen roppyaku nijū en desu.
ごせんろっぴゃくにじゅうえんです。It's 5,620 yen.

d) Ichiman hassen kyūhyaku yonjū ni en desu.
いちまんはっせんきゅうひゃくよんじゅうにえん です。
It's 18,942 yen.

Further practice

1.

a) Sore wa nan desu ka. それはなんですか。

b) Are wa nan desu ka. あれはなんですか。

2.

a) Happyaku en desu. はっぴゃくえんです。

b) Nisen en desu. にせんえんです。

c) Nanasen hyaku en desu. ななせんひゃくえんです。

d) Kyūsen kyūhyaku kyūjū kyū en desu.

きゅうせんきゅうひゃくきゅうじゅうきゅうえんです。

e) Sanman gosen nanahyaku rokujū hachi en desu.

さんまんごせんななひゃくろくじゅうはちえんです。

f) Jū yonman hassen roppyaku en desu.

じゅうよんまんはっせんろっぴゃくえんです。

3.

a) Sandoicchi wo mittsu onegaishimasu.

サンドイッチをみっつおねがいします。

b) Tamago wo itsutsu onegaishimasu.

たまごをいつつおねがいします。

c) Ringo wo muttsu onegaishimasu.

りんごをむっつおねがいします。

d) Sarada wo yottsu onegaishimasu.

サラダをよっつおねがいします。

e) Kēki wo nanatsu onegaishimasu.

ケーキをななつおねがいします。

4.

a) A: Kore wa nan desu ka. これはなんですか。

B: Soba desu. そばです。

A: Sō desu ka. Ja, kore wo onegaishimasu.

そうですか。じゃ、これをおねがいします。

b) Itadakimasu. いただきます。

c) Gochisōsama deshita. ごちそうさまでした。

d) Oishii desu ne. おいしいですね。

e) Sumimasen. Okaikei wo onegaishimasu.

すみません。おかいけいをおねがいします。

f) A: Pan wo yottsu onegaishimasu.

　パンをよっつおねがいします。

　B: Yonhyaku nana jū en desu.

　よんひゃくななじゅうえんです。

g) A: Kēki to kōcha wo onegaishimasu.

　ケーキとこうちゃをおねがいします。

　B: Nana hyaku gojū en desu.

　ななひゃくごじゅうえんです。

h) Hajimemashite. Shirota desu. Hakone daigaku no gakusei desu.
　Yoroshiku onegaishimasu.

　はじめまして。しろたです。はこねだいがくのがくせいです。

　よろしくおねがいします。

Hiragana Reading Quiz 2

1) okāsan (mother)　　2)otōsan (father) 3) onēsan (elder sister) 4) oniisan (elder brother) 5) yūki (courage) 6) bōshi (hat/cap) 7) kitte (postal stamp) 8) zasshi (magazine) 9) shashin (photo) 10) kyūkyūsha (ambulance) 11) shōbōsha (fire engine)

12) kōcha (tea) 13) byōin (hospital) 14) jyagaimo (potato)

15) gyūnyū (milk) 16) hyaku en (100yen) 17) jū en (10yen)

18) ryokō(trip, travel) 19) obentō(bento, lunch box)

20) Tōkyō (Tokyo) 21) Kyōto (Kyoto)

Chapter 3.

Speaking practice

1) Shatsu wo kaitain desu ga. シャツをかいたいんですが。

2) Kuruma wo kaitain desuga. くるまをかいたいんですが。

3) Keshigomu wo futatsu kaitain desuga.

　けしゴムをふたつかいたいんですが。

4) Zasshi wa doko desu ka. ざっしはどこですか。

5) Taburetto wa doko desu ka. タブレットはどこですか。

6) Ikura desu ka. いくらですか。

Listening practice

1) A: Sumimasen. Aisukuriimu wa doko desu ka.

　　すみません。アイスクリームはどこですか。

　　　Excuse me. Where is ice creams?

　B: Aisukuriimu wa gyūnyū uriba no mae desu.

　　アイスクリームはぎゅうにゅううりばのまえです。

　　　Ice creams are in front of milk section.

　A: Arigatō gozaimasu. ありがとうございます。 Thank you.

　Answer: item: ice cream, the place: in front of milk section

2) A: Sumimasen. Biiru wa doko desu ka.

　　すみません。ビールはどこですか。

　　Excuse me. Where is beer?

　B: Biiru wa asoko desu. Wain uriba no migi ni arimasu.

　　ビールはあそこです。ワインうりばのみぎにあります。

　　Beer is over there. It is the right side of wine section.

　A: Arigatō gozaimasu. ありがとうございます。

　　Thank you.

　Answer: item: beer, the place: the right side of wine section

3) A: Sumimasen. Kamera wo kaitain desu ga.

　　すみません。カメラをかいたいんですが。

　　Excuse me. I would like to buy a camera.

　B: Kamera uriba wa yonkai ni gozaimasu.

　　カメラうりばはよんかいにございます。

　　The camera section is on the forth floor.

　A: Arigatō gozaimasu. ありがとうございます。

　　Thank you.

　Answer: item: camera,　the place: the 4th floor

Further practice

1.

a) A: Sumimasen. Bunbōgu wa doko desu ka.

すみません。ぶんぼうぐはどこですか。

B: Rokkai desu. ろっかいです。

b) A: Sumimasen. Kōto wa doko desu ka.

すみません。コートはどこですか。

B: Gokai desu. ごかいです。

c) A: Sumimasen. Wain wa doko desu ka.

すみません。ワインはどこですか。

B: Chika ikkai desu. ちかいっかいです。

2.

a) A: Sumimasen. Kasa wa doko desu ka.

すみません。かさはどこですか。

B: Kaban no shita desu. かばんのしたです。

b) A: Sumimasen. Jisho wa doko desu ka.

すみません。じしょはどこですか。

B: Terebi no mae desu. テレビのまえです。

c) A: Sumimasen. Shinbun wa doko desuka.

すみません。しんぶんはどこですか。

B: Pasokon no ushiro desu. パソコンのうしろです。

d) A: Sumimasen. Tokei wa doko desu ka.

すみません。とけいはどこですか。

B: Keitai denwa no migi desu. けいたいでんわのみぎです。

e) A: Sumimasen. Terebi wa doko desu ka.

すみません。テレビはどこですか。

B: Beddo no hidari desu. ベッドのひだりです。

3.

a) A: Sore wa ikura desu ka. それはいくらですか。

B: Nihyaku en desu. にひゃくえんです。

b) A: Are wa ikura desu ka. あれはいくらですか。

B: Sen en desu. せんえんです。

c) A: Kore wa ikura desu ka. これはいくらですか。

B: Ichiman en desu. いちまんえんです。

d) A: Sore wa ikura desu ka. それはいくらですか。

B: Sen yonhyaku en desu. せんよんひゃくえんです。

e) A: Are wa ikura desu ka. あれはいくらですか。

B: Niman sanzen en desu. にまんさんぜんえんです。

4.
a) Chotto ōkii desu. Mō sukoshi chiisai no wa arimasu ka.
ちょっとおおきいです。もうすこしちいさいのはありますか。
b) Chotto furui desu. Mō sukoshi atarashii no wa arimasu ka.
ちょっとふるいです。もうすこしあたらしいのはありますか。
c) Chotto omoi desu. Mō sukoshi karui no wa arimasu ka.
ちょっとおもいです。もうすこしかるいのはありますか。
d) Chotto takai desu. Mō sukoshi yasui no wa arimasu ka.
ちょっとたかいです。もうすこしやすいのはありますか。

5.
a) A: Sumimasen. Zasshi wa doko desu ka?
すみません。ざっしはどこですか。

B: Zasshi wa achira desu.　ざっしはあちらです。
A: Wakarimashita. Arigatō gozaimasu.
わかりました。ありがとうございます。

b) Hon wa jisho no shita desu.　ほんはじしょのしたです。
c) Keitai denwa wa pasokon no tonari desu.
けいたいでんわはパソコンのとなりです。
d) A: Sumimasen. Kore wa ikura desu ka.
すみません。これはいくらですか。

B: Nisen happyaku en desu.

158

にせんはっぴゃくえんです。

A: Sō desu ka. Chotto takai desu. Mō sukoshi yasui no wa arimasu ka.
そうですか。ちょっとたかいです。もうすこしやすいのは
あります か。

B: Kore wa ikaga desu ka. Sen gohyaku en desu.
これはいかがですか。せんごひゃくえんです。

A: Ii desu ne. いいですね。

e) A: Shichaku shitsu wa doko desu ka.
しちゃくしつはどこですか。

B: Sochira desu. そちらです。

A: Arigatō gozaimasu. ありがとうございます。

f) A: Aisukurīmu wo mittsu onegaishimasu.
アイスクリームをみっつおねがいします。

B: Happyaku nijū en desu. はっぴゃくにじゅうえんです。

Katakana reading Quiz 1

1) Furansu (France)　2) Amerika (America) 3) Itaria (Italy)
4) Roshia (Russia) 5) Kenia (Kenya)　6) Toruko (Turkey)
7) Mekishiko (Mexico) 8) Supein (Spain)　9) Indo (India)
10) wain (wine)　11) koara (koala)　12) panda (panda)
13) raion (lion)　14) terebi (TV) 15) kamera (camera)
16) naifu (knife) 17) shatsu (shirt) 18) zubon (trousers)
19) pen (pen)　20) piza (pizza) 21) pan (bread)

Chapter 4.

Speaking practice

1) A: Yūbinkyoku wa doko desu ka.

ゆうびんきょくはどこですか。

B: Ano shingō wo migi ni magatte kudasai.

あのしんごうをみぎにまがってください。

A: Arigatō gozaimasu. ありがとうございます。

2) A: Bijutsukan wa doko desu ka.

びじゅつかんはどこですか。

B: Kono michi wo massugu itte kudasai. Bijutsukan wa ginkō no migi ni arimasu.

このみちをまっすぐいってください。びじゅつかんはぎん

こうのみぎにあります。

A: Arigatō gozaimasu.ありがとうございます。

3) A: Nagoya eki e ikitain desu ga, hōmu wa doko desu ka.

なごやえきへいきたいんですが、ホームはどこですか。

B: Nagoya hōmen wa gobansen no hōmu desu.

なごやほうめんはごばんせんのホームです。

A: Arigatō gozaimasu.　ありがとうございます。

Listening practice

1) Smith: Sumimasen, Yamadasan. Doyōbi ni Kyōto e ikitain desu ga, dōyatte ikimasu ka.

すみません、やまださん。どようびにきょうとへいき

たいんですが、どうやっていきますか。

Excuse me, Mr.Yamada. I would like to go to Kyoto on Saturday. How do I go there?

Yamada: Tōkyō eki kara Shinkansen de ikimasu.

とうきょうえきからしんかんせんでいきます。

You go by Shinkansen from Tokyo station.

Smith: Arigatō gozaimasu.　ありがとうございます。

Thank you.

Answer: doyōbi, Shinkansen, Kyōto

2) Smith: Sumimasen. Shin-Ōsaka e ikitain desuga, hōmu wa doko desu ka.

すみません。しんおおさかへいきたいんですが、ホームはどこですか。

Excuse me, I would like to go to Shin-Osaka. Where is the platform?

Onna no hito: Shin-Ōsaka hōmen wa jūhachi bansen no hōmu desu.

しんおおさかほうめんはじゅうはちばんせんのホームです。

The platform for Shin-Osaka-bound train is no.18.

Smith: Arigatō gozaimasu.   ありがとうございます。

Answer: Shin-Osaka, 18

3) Smith: Sumimasen. Umeda e ikitain desuga, ikura desu ka.

すみません。うめだへいきたいんですが、いくらですか。

Excuse me. I would like to go to Umeda. How much is it?

Ekiin: Nihyaku yonjū en desu.

にひゃくよんじゅうえんです。It's 240 yen.

Smith: Arigatō gozaimasu.   ありがとうございます。

Thank you.

Answer: Umeda, 240 yen

Further practice

1.

a) Kayōbi ni Yokohama e ikitain desu ga.

かようびによこはまへいきたいんですが。

b) Kinyōbi ni Kyōto e ikitain desu ga.

きんようびにきょうとへいきたいんですが。

c) Mokuyōbi ni Fukuoka e ikitain desu ga.

もくようびにふくおかへいきたいんですが。

d) Doyōbi ni Kanazawa e ikitain desu ga.

どようびにかなざわへいきたいんですが。

e) Getsuyōbi ni Sapporo e ikitain desu ga.

げつようびにさっぽろへいきたいんですが。

f) Suiyōbi ni Sendai e ikitain desu ga.

すいようびにせんだいへいきたいんですが。

g) Nichiyōbi ni Kagawa e ikitain desu ga.

にちようびにかがわへいきたいんですが。

2.

a) Densha de Ginza e ikimasu.

でんしゃでぎんざへいきます。

b) Takushii de Shibuya e ikimasu.

タクシーでしぶやへいきます。

c) Basu de Shinjuku e ikimasu.

バスでしんじゅくへいきます。

d) Kuruma de Nakano e ikimasu.

くるまでなかのへいきます。

e) Chikatetsu de Ueno e ikimasu.

ちかてつでうえのへいきます。

3.

a) Narita de hikōki wo orimasu.

なりたでひこうきをおります。

b) Chiba de basu ni norimasu.

ちばでバスにのります。

c) Yoyogi de takushii wo orimasu.

よよぎでタクシーをおります。

d) Tokushima de fune ni norimasu.

とくしまでふねにのります。

e) Iwami de densha wo orimasu.

いわみででんしゃをおります。

4.

a) Shingō wo migi ni magatte kudasai.

しんごうをみぎにまがってください。

b) Ano kado wo hidari ni magatte kudasai.

あのかどをひだりにまがってください。

c) Kono michi wo massugu itte kudasai.

このみちをまっすぐいってください。

d) Ano shingō wo hidari ni magatte kudasai.

あのしんごうをひだりにまがってください。

5.

a) A: Sumimasen. Yonago eki e ikitain desu ga, ikura desu ka.

すみません。よなごえきへいきたいんですが、いくらです
か。

B: 15,000 (ichiman gosen) en desu. いちまんごせんえんです。

b) A: Sumimasen. Toyama eki e ikitain desu ga, ikura desu ka.

すみません。とやまえきへいきたいんですが、いくらです
か。

B: 2,600 (nisen roppyaku) en desu. にせんろっぴゃくえんです。

c) A: Sumimasen. Nara eki e ikitain desu ga, ikura desu ka. すみませ
ん。ならえきへいきたいんですが、いくらですか。

B: 580 (gohyaku hachijū) en desu. ごひゃくはちじゅうえんです。

6.

a) B: Rokugatsu yokka desu.　ろくがつよっかです。

b) B: Kugatsu nanoka desu.　くがつなのかです。

c) B: Jūnigatsu muika desu.　じゅうにがつむいかです。

d) B: Sangatsu yōka desu.　さんがつようかです。

e) (Please answer your own birthday!)

7.

a) A: Tanjōbi wa itsu desu ka. たんじょうびはいつですか。

B: Jūgatsu jūyokka desu.　じゅうがつじゅうよっかです。

b) A: Kyō wa nanyōbi desu ka.　きょうはなんようびですか。

B: Mokuyōbi desu.　もくようびです。

c) A: Sumimasen. Ginza e ikitain desu ga, ikura desu ka.

すみません。ぎんざへいきたいんですが、いくらですか。

B: Nihyaku sanjū en desu.　にひゃくさんじゅうえんです。

d) A: Jinja wa doko desu ka.　じんじゃはどこですか。

B: Ano kōsaten wo massugu itte kudasai.

あのこうさてんをまっすぐいってください。

e) A: Kōen wa doko desu ka.　こうえんはどこですか。

B: Kōban no tonari desu.　こうばんのとなりです。

f) A: Sumimasen. Shashin wo onegaishimasu.

すみません。しゃしんをおねがいします。

B: Ii desu yo.　いいですよ。

Katakana Reading Quiz 2 (Optional)

1) banana (banana) 2) painappuru (pineapple) 3) mangō (mango)
4) kyabetsu (cabbage)　5)gurēpufurūtsu (grapefruit) 6) konpyūtā
(computer) 7) herikoputā (helicopter) 8)Igirisu (UK) 9) Kanada
(Canada) 10) gitā (guitar)　11) gēmu (game) 12) Oranda
(Holland) 13) chokorēto (chocolate) 14) Barentaindē (Valentin's
day) 15) biora (viola) 16) Ōsutoria (Austria) 17) kēki (cake)
18) aisukuriimu (ice cream) 19) kōhii (coffee) 20) furūto (flute)
21) poketto (pocket)

Chapter 5.

Speaking practice

1) Atama ga itai desu. あたまがいたいです。

Kata no chōshi ga warui desu.　かたのちょうしがわるいです。

Samuke ga shimasu.　さむけがします。

2) You: Sumimasen. Koshi ga itain desu ga.

すみません。こしがいたいんですが。

Hotel staff: Daijōbu desu ka. だいじょうぶですか。

You: Kusuriya e ikitain desu ga.

くすりやへいきたいんですが。

Hotel staff: Kono michi wo massugu itte kudasai. Kusuriya wa panya no tonari desu.

このみちをまっすぐいってください。くすりやはパンや のとなりです。

You: Arigatō gozaimasu. ありがとうございます。

Listening practice

1) A: Sumimasen. Kuruma no chōshi ga waruin desu ga.

すみません。くるまのちょうしがわるいんですが。

Excuse me. There is something wrong with my car.

B: Sō desu ka. Sugu ni naoshi masu.

そうですか。すぐになおします。I see. I'll soon fix it.

A: Onegaishimasu. おねがいします。Please.

2) A: Sumimasen. Pasokon no chōshi ga waruin desu ga.

すみません。パソコンのちょうしがわるいんですが。

B: Wakarimashita. Sugu ni naoshimasu.

わかりました。すぐになおします。

OK. I'll fix it soon.

A: Onegaishimasu. おねがいします。Please.

3) A: Sumimasen. Seki ga derun desu ga.

すみません。せきがでるんですが。

Excuse me. I have a cough.

B: Kono kusuri wa ikaga desu ka. Seki ni ii desu.

このくすりはいかがですか。せきにいいです。

How about this medicine? It is good for cough.

A: Arigatō gozaimasu. ありがとうございます。 Thank you.

4) A: Sumimasen. Nodo ga itain desu ga.

すみません。のどがいたいんですが。

Excuse me. I have a sore throat.

B: Sō desu ne. Kono kusuri ga nodo ni ii desu yo.

そうですね。このくすりがのどにいいですよ。

Let me see. This medicine is good for your throat.

A: Arigatō gozaimasu. ありがとうございます。 Thank you.

5) A: Sumimasen. Netsu ga arun desu ga.

すみません。ねつがあるんですが。

Excuse me. I have a fever.

B: Netsu desu ka. Kono kusuri ga netsu ni ii desu yo.

ねつですか。このくすりがねつにいいですよ。

You have a fever, do you? This medicine is good for a fever.

A: Arigatō gozaimasu. ありがとうございます。 Thank you.

6) A: Sumimasen. Onaka no chōshi ga waruin desu ga.

すみません。おなかのちょうしがわるいんですが。

Excuse me. I have an upset stomach.

B: Kono kusuri wa ikaga desu ka. Onaka ni ii desu.

このくすりはいかがですか。おなかにいいです。

How about this medicine? It is good for the stomach.

A: Arigatō gozaimasu. ありがとうございます。 Thank you.

Further practice

1.

a) Kuruma no chōshi ga waruin desu ga.

くるまのちょうしがわるいんですが。

There is something wrong with the car.

b) Karada no chōshi ga waruin desu ga.

からだのちょうしがわるいんですが。 I'm not well.

c) Me no chōshi ga waruin desu ga.

めのちょうしがわるいんですが。

There is something wrong with my eye(s).

d) Onaka no chōshi ga waruin desu ga.

おなかのちょうしがわるいんですが。

I have an upset stomach.

e) Terebi no chōshi ga waruin desu ga.

テレビのちょうしがわるいんですが。

There is something wrong with the TV.

f) Keitai denwa no chōshi ga waruin desu ga.

けいたいでんわのちょうしがわるいんですが。

There is something wrong with the mobile phone.

g) Pasokon no chōshi ga waruin desu ga.

パソコンのちょうしがわるいんですが。

There is something wrong with the PC.

2.

a) Onaka ga itai desu.　おなかがいたいです。

b) Atama ga itai desu.　あたまがいたいです。

c) Hanamizu ga demasu.　はなみずがでます。

d) Hakike ga shimasu.　はきけがします。

e) Memai ga shimasu.　めまいがします。

f) Seki ga demasu.　せきがでます。

g) Ude ga itai desu.　うでがいたいです。

h) Hiza ga itai desu.　ひざがいたいです。

i) Samuke ga shimasu.　さむけがします。

3.

a) Ichiji desu.　いちじです。

b) Yoji desu.　よじです。

c) Jūniji desu.　じゅうにじです。

d) Shichiji desu.　しちじです。

e) Kuji desu.　くじです。

f) Sanji juppun desu.　さんじじゅっぷんです。

g) Goji nijuppun desu.　ごじにじゅっぷんです。

h) Jūichiji yonjuppun desu.　じゅういちじよんじゅっぷんです。

i) Rokuji sanjuppun desu. / Rokuji han desu.
　ろくじさんじゅっぷんです。/ろくじはんです。

j) Hachiji gojuppun desu.　はちじごじゅっぷんです。

l) Jūji gofun desu.　じゅうじごふんです。

m) Niji jūgofun desu.　にじじゅうごふんです。

n) Yoji yonpun desu.　よじよんぷんです。

o) Shichiji nanafun desu.　しちじななふんです。

p) Kuji kyūfun desu.　くじきゅうふんです。

4.
a) Ano kōsaten wo migi ni magatte kudasai.
　あのこうさてんをみぎにまがってください。

b) Kono kado wo hidari ni magatte kudasai.
　このかどをひだりにまがってください。

c) Kono michi wo massugu itte kudasai.
　このみちをまっすぐいってください。

d) Ano shingō wo massugu itte kudasai.
　あのしんごうをまっすぐいってください。

5.
a) A: Hakubutsukan wa doko desu ka.
　　はくぶつかんはどこですか。

　B: Toshokan no tonari desu.　としょかんのとなりです。
　or
　　Toshokan no tonari ni arimasu.
　　としょかんのとなりにあります。

b) A: Panya wa doko desu ka.　パンやはどこですか。

　B: Dōbutsuen no mae desu.　どうぶつえんのまえです。
　or
　　Dōbutsuen no mae ni arimasu.
　　どうぶつえんのまえにあります。

c) A: Pūru wa doko desu ka. プールはどこですか。

   B: Hakkai desu. はっかいです。

   or

      Hakkai ni arimasu. はっかいにあります。

6.

a) A: Sumimasen. Sumāto fon no chōshi ga waruin desu ga.

   すみません。スマートフォンのちょうしがわるいんですが。

   B: Sō desu ka. Sugu ni naoshimasu.

   そうですか。すぐになおします。

   A: Onegaishimasu. おねがいします。

b) A: Shigoto no chōshi wa dō desu ka.

   しごとのちょうしはどうですか。

   B: Totemo ii desu. とてもいいです。

c) A: Sumimasen. Nodo ga itain desu ga.

   すみません。のどがいたいんですが。

   B: Daijōbu desu ka. だいじょうぶですか。

   A: Kusuri ga hoshiin desu ga. くすりがほしいんですが。

   B: Kono kusuri wa ikaga desu ka. Nodo no itami ni ii desu.

   このくすりはいかがですか。のどのいたみにいいです。

   A: Arigatō gozaimasu. ありがとうございます。

d) A: Itsu Sapporo e ikimasu ka. いつさっぽろへいきますか。

   B: Raishū ikimasu. らいしゅういきます。

e) A: Toire wa doko desu ka. トイレはどこですか。

   B: Toire wa nikai desu. トイレはにかいです。

or   Toire wa nikai ni arimasu. トイレはにかいにあります。

Final Hiragana and Katakana Reading Quiz

1) Chūgoku (China)   2) Hajimemashite (How do you do?)
3) burokkorii (broccoli) 4) kagi (key)   5) bōrupen (ballpoint pen)
6) hasami (scissors) 7) ringo (apple) 8) sētā (sweater) 9) tomato
(tomato) 10) asuparagasu (asparagus) 11) pasokon (PC) 12)
torakku (truck, lorry) 13) neko (cat) 14) jisho (dictionary) 15)
zerii (jelly) 16) taiko (drum)   17) patokā (police car)   18) fōku
(fork) 19) Konnichiwa (hello)   20) Arigatō gozaimasu (Thank you)
21) Sayōnara (good bye)

About the Author

Dr. Asuka Tsuchiya is an award-winning psychologist, qualified Japanese teacher, #1 best-selling author, and mother with two adorable kids.

She majored in Linguistics and Literature at the University of Tokyo. She received her MA in Education at the Graduate School of Education at the University of Tokyo. During this period, she was also trained as a psychotherapist.

After working as a psychotherapist in both the educational and the medical fields, she started studying human communications at the Graduate School of Humanities and Sciences at Nara Women's University. She received her Ph.D. in Psychology as well as the Best Postgraduate Student Award. Her Ph. D work was awarded the "Association of Japanese Clinical Psychology Encouragement Prize" from the Association of Japanese Clinical Psychology, Japan's most prominent psychological association.

Asuka sensei is now teaching Japanese in the UK, having qualified through the Japan Educational Exchanges and Services (JEES) organization, the most prestigious Japanese teaching authority in Japan. She provides high-quality Japanese teaching based on her profound knowledge of the Japanese language and education. And, as a professional psychologist and psychotherapist, she helps learners have more confidence in speaking Japanese.

Currently, she runs communicative and engaging Japanese lessons at multiple locations, including the University of Southampton. She's published Japanese language textbooks for students and teachers and got No.1 in various best-sellers rankings in Amazon US, UK, and Japan.

Japanese-English Glossary

A

achira, あちら, over there (polite), 66

achira, あちら, that (far) direction, 100

Airurando, アイルランド, Ireland, 24

aisukuriimu, アイスクリーム, ice cream, 51

aki, あき, autumn, 151

amari yokunai desu, あまりよくないです, not so good, 124

amari, あまり, not so much, 130

Amerika jin, アメリカじん, American, 20

Amerika, アメリカ, America, 17

anata, あなた, you, 20

ano, あの, ah, 11

ano, あの, that, 100

ano, あの, um, 103

are, あれ, that (far), 36

arerugii, アレルギー, allegy, 133

arigatō gozaimashita, ありがとうございました, thank you (past tense), 42

arigatō gozaimasu, ありがとうございます, Thank you, 22

arimasu, あります, be, exist, there is/are (for non- living), 65

ashi, あし, leg, feet, 133

ashita, あした, tomorrow, 112

asoko, あそこ, over there, 65

asuparagasu, アスパラガス, asparagus, 169

atama, あたま, head, 132

atarashii, あたらしい, new, 79

ato, あと, after, 103

B

banana, バナナ, banana, 52

bansen, ばんせん, platform no., 99

Barentaindē, バレンタインデー, Valentin's day, 163

basu, バス, bus, 93

basutei, バスてい, bus stop, 107

beddo, ベッド, bed, 82

bengoshi, べんごし, lawyer, 23

benkyō, べんきょう, study, 131

benpi, べんぴ, constipation, 134

betsubetsu, べつべつ, separately, 42

biiru, ビール, beer, 50

bijutsukan, びじゅつかん, art gallery, 106

biora, ビオラ, viola, 163

biru, ビル, building, 91

biyōshi, びようし, hairdresser, 23

bōrupen, ボールペン, ballpoint pen, 81

bōshi, ぼうし, hat, cap, 154

budō, ぶどう, grapes, 52

bunbōgu, ぶんぼうぐ, stationary, 81

Burajiru jin, ブラジルじん, Brazilian, 24

Burajiru, ブラジル, Brazil, 24

burokkorii, ブロッコリー, broccoli, 169

eigakan, えいがかん, cinema, 106

Ejiputo jin, エジプトじん, Egyptian, 24

Ejiputo, エジプト, Egypt, 24

eki, えき, station, 91

en, えん, Japanese yen, 42

enjinia, エンジニア, enjineer, 23

enpitsu, えんぴつ, pencil, 37, 81

etto, えっと, uh, 65

F

fāsto fūdo, ファーストフード, fast food shop, 46

fōku, フォーク, fork, 7

fune, ふね, ship, 93

Furansu jin, フランスじん, French, 24

Furansu ryōri, フランスりょうり, French cuisine, 51

Furansu, フランス, France, 24

furui, ふるい, old (cannot use it for living things), 79

furūto, フルート, flute, 163

futatsu, ふたつ, two things (general counter), 46

futsuka yoi, ふつかよい, hangover, 134

futsuka, ふつか, the 2nd day, 110

fuyu, ふゆ, winter, 151

G

ga, が, particle (indicating subject), 35

- ga hoshiin desu ga, 〜がほしいんですが, I want -, 130

gaka, がか, painter, 23

gakkō, がっこう, school, 107

gakusei, がくせい, student, 17

gēmu, ゲーム, game, 163

geri, げり, diarrhea, 134

getsuyōbi, げつようび, Monday, 108

ginkō, ぎんこう, bank, 17

ginkōin, ぎんこういん, bank clerk, 23

gitā, ギター, guitar, 163

go, ご, 5, 53

gō, ごう, (counters for clothes size), 76

gochisō samadeshita, ごちそうさまでした, (said after eating a meal), 42

gofun, ごふん, 5 minutes, 136

gogatsu, ごがつ, May, 109

gohan, ごはん, rice, 50

gohyaku, ごひゃく, 500, 55

goissho, ごいっしょ, together (polite), 42

goji, ごじ, 5: 00, 135

gojū, ごじゅう, 50, 54

gojuppun, ごじゅっぷん, 50 minutes, 136

gokai, ごかい, 5th floor, 73

goman, ごまん, 50,000, 56

gosen, ごせん, 5,000, 55

gozaimasu, ございます, there is (politer expression of, 70

gurēpufurūtsu, グレープフルーツ, grapefruit, 163

gyūniku, ぎゅうにく, beef, 51

gyūnū, ぎゅうにゅう, milk, 50

H

ha, は, tooth, 132

I

ikaga desu ka, いかがですか, how about … ? (polite), 46

ikimasu, いきます, go, 91

ikkai, いっかい, 1st floor, 72

ikura, いくら, how much, 76

ima, いま, now, 136

imasu, います, be, exist, there is/are (for living), 65

Indo jin, インドじん, Indian, 24

Indo, インド, India, 24

Indoneshia jin, インドネシアじん, Indonesian, 24

Indoneshia, インドネシア, Indonesia, 24

inu, いぬ, dog, 151

ippun, いっぷん, 1 minute, 135

irasshaimase, いらっしゃいませ, welcome (used by shop clerk or restaurant staff), 35

isha, いしゃ, medical doctor, 23

isu, いす, chair, 82

itadakimasu, いただきます, (said before eating a meal), 42

itai, いたい, painful, 125

Itaria jin, イタリアじん, Italian, 24

Itaria ryōri, イタリアりょうり, Italian cuisine, 51

Itaria, イタリア, Italy, 24

itchō, いっちょう, 1,000,000,000,000, 57

itsu, いつ, when, 112

itsuka, いつか, the 5th day, 110

itsutsu, いつつ, five things (general counter), 48

itte kudasai, いってください, please go, 91

J

ja, じゃ, well then, 35

jagaimo, じゃがいも, potato, 52

jaketto, ジャケット, jacket, 82

jidōhanbaiki, じどうはんばいき, vending machine, 99

jiinzu, ジーンズ, jeans, 82

jin, じん, person from, 17

jinja, じんじゃ, Shinto shrine, 106

jisho, じしょ, dictionary, 81

jūgatsu, じゅうがつ, October, 109

jūgogō, じゅうごう, size15, 78

jūgonichi, じゅうごにち, the 15th day, 111

jūhachinichi, じゅうはちにち, the 18th day, 111

jūichigatsu, じゅういちがつ, November, 110

jūichigō, じゅういちごう, size11, 77

jūichiji, じゅういちじ, 11: 00, 135

jūichinichi, じゅういちにち, the 11th day, 111

jūji, じゅうじ, 10: 00, 135

jukkai, じゅっかい, 10th floor, 73

jūkunichi, じゅうくにち, the 19th day, 111

jūman, じゅうまん, 100,000, 56

jūnigatsu, じゅうにがつ, December, 110

jūniji, じゅうにじ, 12: 00, 135

jūninichi, じゅうににち, the 12th day, 111

jūoku, じゅうおく, 1,000,000,000, 57

juppun, じゅっぷん, 10 minutes, 136

jūrokunichi, じゅうろくにち, the 16th day, 111

K

M

nifun, にふん, 2 minutes, 135

nigatsu, にがつ, February, 109

Nihon, にほん, Japan, 24

Nihongo, にほんご, Japanese language, 131

Nihon jin, にほんじん, Japanese, 24

Nihon ryōri, にほんりょうり, Japanese cuisine, 51

nihyaku, にひゃく, 200, 54

niji, にじ, 2: 00, 135

nijū, にじゅう, 20, 54

nijūgonichi, にじゅうごにち, the 25th day, 111

nijūhachinichi, にじゅうはちにち, the 28th day, 111

nijūichinichi, にじゅういちにち, the 21st day, 111

nijūkunichi, にじゅうくにち, the 29th day, 111

nijūninichi, にじゅうににち, the 22nd day, 111

nijuppun, にじゅっぷん, 20 minutes, 136

nijūrokunichi, にじゅうろくにち, the 26th day, 111

nijūsannichi, にじゅうさんにち, the 23rd day, 111

nijūshichinichi, にじゅうしちにち, the 27th day, 111

nijūyokka, にじゅうよっか, the 24th day, 111

nikai, にかい, 2nd floor, 72

niku, にく, meat, 51

nikuya, にくや, butcher, 107

niman, にまん, 20,000, 56

ninjin, にんじん, carrot, 52

nisen, にせん, 2,000, 55

nizakana, にざかな, stewed fish, 51

no, の, one, 76

no, の, particle (of), 17

nodo, のど, throat, 130

nomemasen, のめません, cannot drink, 133

nomimono, のみもの, drinks, 50

norimono yoi, のりものよい, motion sickness, 134

nōto, ノート, notebook, 81

Nyūjiirando jin, ニュージーランドじん, New Zealander, 25

Nyūjiirando, ニュージーランド, New Zealand, 25

Nyūyōku, ニューヨーク, New York, 27

O

obentō, おべんとう, lunch box, 154

ocha, おちゃ, green tea, 50

ochawan, おちゃわん, rice bowl, 60

Ohayō gozaimasu, おはようございます, Good morning, 22

oishii, おいしい, delicious, 42

okaikei, おかいけい, bill, 42

okāsan, おかあさん, mother, 154

ōkii, おおきい, big, 6

okimari desu ka, おきまりですか, have you decided on your order? (polite), 46

omachi kudasai, おまちください, please wait (polite), 42

omeshiagari, おめしあがり, to eat (polite), 46

omochi kudasai, おもちください, please take (polite), 42

omoi, おもい, heavy, 79

onaka, おなか, tummy, stomach, 125

P

R

ryōri, りょうり, dish, 51

(country name) ryōri, (country name) りょうり, (country) dish, 51

S

saisen bako, さいせんばこ, offering box, 118

sakana, さかな, fish, 51

sakanaya, さかなや, fishmonger, 107

sakaya, さかや, liquor shop, 107

sake, さけ, salmon, 51

sakka, さっか, author, 23

samuke, さむけ, chill, 127

san, さん, 3, 53

san, さん, Mr, Mrs, Ms, Miss (add after a person's name), 11

sanbyaku, さんびゃく, 300, 54

sandoicchi, サンドイッチ, sandwich, 50

sangai, さんがい, 3rd floor, 70

sangatsu, さんがつ, March, 109

sanji, さんじ, 3: 00, 135

sanjū, さんじゅう, 30, 54

sanjūichinichi, さんじゅういちにち, the 31st day, 112

sanjūnighi, さんじゅうにち, the 30th day, 112

sanjuppun, さんじゅっぷん, 30 minutes, 136

sanman, さんまん, 30,000, 56

sanmon, さんもん, gate of Buddhism temple, 119

sanpun, さんぷん, 3 minutes, 135

sanzen, さんぜん, 3,000, 55

sarada, サラダ, salad, 50

sashimi, さしみ, sashimi (sliced raw fish), 35

satsumaimo, さつまいも, sweet potato, 52

sayōnara, さようなら, good bye, 22

seijika, せいじか, politician, 23

seiritsū, せいりつう, period pains, 134

seki, せき, cough, 127

sen, せん, 1,000, 55

senaka, せなか, back, 133

sengetsu, せんげつ, last month, 112

senman, せんまん, 10,000,000, 57

senoku, せんおく, 100,000,000,000, 57

sensei, せんせい, teacher, 22

senshū, せんしゅう, last week, 112

sētā, セーター, sweater, 82

shāpu penshiru, シャープペンシル, mechanical pencil, 81

shashin, しゃしん, photograph, 103

shatsu, シャツ, shirt, 82

shawā, シャワー, shower, 122

shichaku shimasu, しちゃくします, try on, 76

shichaku shite mo ii desu ka, しちゃくしてもいいですか, May I try it on?, 76

shichaku shitsu, しちゃくしつ, fitting room, 76

shichi, しち, 7, 53

shichigatsu, しちがつ, July, 109

shichiji, しちじ, 7: 00, 135

shigatsu, しがつ, April, 109

shima, しま, island, 151

shinbun, しんぶん, newspaper, 81

T

Z

English-Japanese Glossary

0

0, zero, ゼロ, 52

1

1, ichi, いち, 39

10, jū, じゅう, 53

100, hyaku, ひゃく, 54

1,000, sen, せん, 55

10,000, ichiman, いちまん, 55

100,000, jūman, じゅうまん, 56

1,000,000, hyakuman, ひゃくまん, 56

10,000,000, senman, せんまん, 57

100,000,000, ichioku, いちおく, 57

1,000,000,000, jūoku, じゅうおく, 57

10,000,000,000, hyakuoku, ひゃくおく, 57

100,000,000,000, senoku, せんおく, 57

1,000,000,000,000, itchō, いっちょう, 57

1st floor, ikkai, いっかい, 72

10th floor, jukkai, じゅっかい, 73

2

2, ni, に, 43

20, nijū, にじゅう, 54

200, nihyaku, にひゃく, 54

2,000, nisen, にせん, 55

20,000, niman, にまん, 56

2nd floor, nikai, にかい, 72

3

3, san, さん, 53

30, sanjū, さんじゅう, 54

300, sanbyaku, さんびゃく, 54

3,000, sanzen, さんぜん, 55

30, 000, sanman, さんまん, 56

3rd floor, sangai, さんがい, 70

4

4, yon, よん, shi, し, 53

40, yonjū, よんじゅう, 54

400, yonhyaku, よんひゃく, 55

4,000, yonsen, よんせん, 55

40,000, yonman, よんまん, 56

4th floor, yonkai, よんかい, 73

5

5, go, ご, 53

50, gojū, ごじゅう, 54

500, gohyaku, ごひゃく, 55

5,000, gosen, ごせん, 55

50,000, goman, ごまん, 56

5th floor, gokai, ごかい, 73

6

6, roku, ろく, 53

60, rokujū, ろくじゅう, 54

B

back (body), senaka, せなか, 133

back (behind), ushiro, うしろ, 68

bad, warui, わるい, 122

bag, kaban, かばん, 82

bakery, panya, パンや, 107

ballpoint pen, bōrupen, ボールペン, 81

banana, banana, バナナ, 52

bank clerk, ginkōin, ぎんこういん, 23

bank, ginkō, ぎんこう, 17

basement 1st floor, chika ikkai, ちか いっかい, 73

be working, hataraite imasu, はたら いています, 17

be, exist, there is/are (for living), imasu, います, 65

be, exist, there is/are (for non- living), arimasu, あります, 65

bed, beddo, ベッド, 82

beef, gyūniku, ぎゅうにく, 51

beer, biiru, ビール, 50

Beijing, Pekin, ペキン, 27

big: ōkii, おおきい, 6

bill, okaikei, おかいけい, 42

birthday, tanjōbi, たんじょうび, 112

black, kuroi, くろい, 91

blowing one's nose, hana wo kamu, はなをかむ, 142

body, karada, からだ, 132

bone, hone, ほね, 133

book shop, honya, ほんや, 107

book, hon, ほん, 81

boots, būtsu, ブーツ, 82

Brazil, Burajiru, ブラジル, 24

bread, pan, パン, 50

broccoli, burokkorii, ブロッコリー, 169

Buddhist temple, otera, おてら, 106

building, biru, ビル, 72

bus stop, basutei, バスてい, 107

bus, basu, バス, 93

but, demo, でも, 52

butcher, nikuya, にくや, 107

C

cabbage, kyabetsu, キャベツ, 163

café, kafe, カフェ, 107

cake, kēki, ケーキ, 51

call, yobimasu, よびます, 125

came, kimashita, きました, 17

camera, kamera, カメラ, 81

Canada, Kanada, カナダ, 24

cannot drink, nomemase, のめませ ん, 133

cannot eat, taberaremasen, たべら れません, 133

cap, bōshi, ぼうし, 154

car, kuruma, くるま, 82

card, kādo, カード, 81

carrot, ninjin, にんじん, 52

cash desk, reji, レジ, 42

cat, neko, ねこ, 169

chair, isu, いす, 82

change (a train), -ni norikaemasu, 〜 にのりかえます, 91

change (from a subway to a train 1), -kara-ni norikaemasu, 〜から〜に のりかえます, 94

D

E

eraser, keshigomu, けしゴム, 81

excuse me, sumimasen, すみません, 11

expensive, takai, たかい, 76

eye, me, め, 132

F

face, kao, かお, 132

fast food shop, fāsuto fūdo, ファーストフード, 46

father, otōsan, おとうさん, 6

February, nigatsu, にがつ, 109

fever, netsu, ねつ, 126

finger, yubi, ゆび, 132

fire engine, shōbōsha, しょうぼうしゃ, 154

fire station, shōbōsho, しょうぼうしょ, 106

fish, sakana, さかな, 51

fishmonger, sakanaya, さかなや, 107

fitting room, shichaku shitsu, しちゃくしつ, 76

fix, naoshimasu, なおします, 122

flower, hana, はな, 151

flute, furūto, フルート, 163

foods, tabemono, たべもの, 50

foot, ashi, あし, 133

fork, fōku, フォーク, 7

France, Furansu, フランス, 24

French cuisine, furansu ryōri, フランスりょうり, 51

Friday, kinyōbi, きんようび, 108

friend, tomodachi, ともだち, 17

from (particle indicating origin or point of departure), kara, から, 17

from, kara, から, 91

front, mae, まえ, 68

fruit, kudamono, くだもの, 52

G

game, gēmu, ゲーム, 163

general counters (special number for counting things), 47

Germany, Doitsu, ドイツ, 24

get off (a train), (densha wo) orimasu, (でんしゃを) おります, 91

get on (a train), (desha ni) norimasu, (でんしゃに) のります, 94

go, ikimasu, いきます, 91

good bye, sayōnara, さようなら, 22

good evening, konbanwa, こんばんは, 22

good morning, ohayō gozaimasu, おはようございます, 22

good night, oyasumi nasai, おやすみなさい, 22

good, ii, いい, 123

grapefruit, gurēpufurūtsu, グレープフルーツ, 163

grapes, budō, ぶどう, 52

great, totemo ii desu, とてもいいです, 124

green tea, ocha, おちゃ, 50

grilled fish, yakizakana, やきざかな, 35

grilled meat, yakiniku, やきにく, 51

guitar, gitā, ギター, 163

H

hair, kami, かみ, 132

hairdresser, biyōshi, びようし, 23

hamburger, hanbāgā, ハンバーガー, 50

hand, te, て, 132

hangover, futsuka yoi, ふつかよい, 134

have you decided on your order? (polite), okimari desu ka, おきまりですか, 46

hat, bōshi, ぼうし, 154

head, atama, あたま, 132

heavy, omoi, おもい, 79

helicopter, herikoputā, ヘリコプター, 163

hello, konnichiwa, こんにちは, 22

here, koko, ここ, 66

heyfever, kafunshō, かふんしょう, 134

Hong Kong, Honkon, ほんこん, 24

hospital, byōin, びょういん, 23

hotdog, hotto doggu, ホットドッグ, 50

hotel, hoteru, ホテル, 91

housewife, shufu, しゅふ, 23

how about ... ? (polite), ikaga desu ka, いかがですか, 46

how do you do?, hajimemashite, はじめまして, 13

How is ...?, dō desu ka, どうですか, 124

how much, ikura, いくら, 76

how, dōyatte, どうやって, 91

I

I am sorry (polite), mōshiwake gozaimasen, もうしわけございません, 122

I see, sō desu ka, そうですか, 17

I want -, - ga hoshiin desu ga, ～がほしいんですが, 130

I would like to buy, kaitain desu ga, かいたいんですが, 70

I would like to go to, -e ikitain desu ga, ～へ いきたいんですが, 91

I, watashi, わたし, 14

ice cream, aisukuriimu, アイスクリーム, 51

immediately, sugu ni, すぐに, 122

incense sticks, osenkō, おせんこう, 119

India, Indo, インド, 24

Indonesia, Indoneshia, インドネシア, 24

inside a shop, tennai, てんない, 46

inside, middle, naka, なか, 68

Ireland, Airurando, アイルランド, 24

island, shima, しま, 151

Italian cuisine, Itaria ryōri, イタリアりょうり, 51

Italy, Itaria, イタリア, 24

J

jacket, jaketto, ジャケット, 82

January, ichigatsu, いちがつ, 109

Japan, Nihon, にほん, 24

Japanese cuisine, nihon ryōri にほんりょうり, 51

Japanese language, Nihongo, にほん
ご, 131

Japanese yen, en, えん, 42

jelly, zerii, ゼリー, 169

jū, じゅう, 10

juice, jūsu, ジュース, 50

July, shichigatsu, しちがつ, 109

junction, kōsaten, こうさてん, 94

June, rokugatsu, ろくがつ, 109

K

Kenya, Kenia, ケニア, 158

key, kagi, かぎ, 169

knee, hiza, ひざ, 133

knife, naifu, ナイフ, 158

koala, koara, コアラ, 158

Kyoto, Kyōto, きょうと, 154

L

last month, sengetsu, せんげつ, 112

last week. senshū, せんしゅう, 112

last year, kyonen, きょねん, 112

lawyer, bengoshi, べんごし, 23

left, hidari, ひだり, 68

leg, ashi, あし, 133

library, toshokan, としょかん, 106

light, karui, かるい, 79

lion, raion, ライオン, 158

liquor shop, sakaya, さかや, 107

lorry, torakku, トラック, 169

lower back, koshi, こし, 133

lunch box, obentō, おべんとう, 154

M

magazine, zasshi, ざっし, 81

mango, mangō, マンゴー, 163

March, sangatsu, さんがつ, 109

may I help you? (used by shop clerk
or restaurant staff), irasshaimase,
いらっしゃいませ, 35

May I try it on?, shichaku shite mo ii
desu ka, しちゃくしてもいいで
すか, 76

May, gogatsu, ごがつ, 109

meal set, teishoku, ていしょく, 35

meat, niku, にく, 51

mechanical pencil, shāpu penshiru, シ
ャープペンシル, 81

medical doctor, isha, いしゃ, 23

medicine, kusuri, くすり, 130

menu, menyū, メニュー, 35

Mexico, Mekishiko, メキシコ, 25

milk, miruku, ミルク, gyūnū, ぎゅう
にゅう, 50

miso soup, misoshiru, みそしる, 35

mobile phone, keitai denwa, けいた
いでんわ, 82

Monday, getsuyōbi, げつようび, 108

mother, okāsan, おかあさん, 154

motion sickness, norimono yoi, のり
ものよい, 134

mountain, yama, やま, 151

mouth, kuchi, くち, 132

Mr, Mrs, Ms, Miss, san, さん, 11

museum, hakubutsukan, はくぶつか
ん, 106

musician, ongakuka, おんがくか, 23

N

nail, tsume, つめ, 132

nauseous, hakike, はきけ, 127

near, in the vicinity, chikaku, ちかく, 68

neck, kubi, くび, 132

New York, Nyūyōku, ニューヨーク, 27

New Zealand, Nyūjiirando, ニュージーランド, 25

new, atarashii, あたらしい, 79

newspaper, shinbun, しんぶん, 81

next month, raigetsu, らいげつ, 112

next to, tonari, となり, 52

next week, raishū, らいしゅう, 112

next year, rainen, らいねん, 112

nice to meet you, dōzo yoroshiku onegaishimasu, どうぞよろしくおねがいします, 13

no, iie, いいえ, 11

nose, hana, はな, 132

not so good, amari yokunai desu, あまりよくないです, 124

not so much, amari, あまり, 130

notebook, nōto, ノート, 81

November, jūichigatsu, じゅういちがつ, 110

now, ima, いま, 136

nurse, kangoshi, かんごし, 23

nut, nattsu, ナッツ, 133

O

October, jūgatsu, じゅうがつ, 109

of, no, の, 17

offering box, saisen bako, さいせんばこ, 118

Oh, really?, sō desu ka, そうですか, 43

OK. I'll do it for you, ii desu yo, いいですよ., 103

old, furui, ふるい, (cannot use it for living things), 79

one, no, の, 76

onion, tamanegi, たまねぎ, 52

orange, mikan, みかん, 52

over there, asoko, あそこ, 65

over there (polite), achira, あちら, 76

P

painful, itai, いたい, 125

painter, gaka, がか, 23

panda, panda, パンダ, 158

Paris, Pari, パリ, 27

park, kōen, こうえん, 106

parking lot, chūshajō, ちゅうしゃじょう, 106

particle (by means of), de, で, 91

particle (by), de, で, 46

particle (indicating a direction), e, へ, 92

particle (indicating object), wo, を, 35

particle (indicating place), ni, に, 68

particle (indicating subject), ga, が, 35

particle (indicating the arrival place of the movement), ni, に, 94

particle (indicating the location where an action takes place), de, で, 17

particle (indicating time), ni, に, 91

particle (isn't it? right?), ne, ね, 42

T

U

Made in United States
Orlando, FL
28 November 2022

25156670R00115